JONATHAN EDWARDS

&

THE VISIBILITY
OF GOD

JAMES CARSE

JONATHAN EDWARDS

&

THE VISIBILITY
OF GOD

CHARLES SCRIBNER'S SONS · NEW YORK

This book is dedicated to the memory
of my father,
JAMES BRADLEY CARSE,
a brilliant maker of histories,
for he knew how to love a boy.

ACKNOWLEDGMENTS

No one can do any research into the thought of Jonathan Edwards without putting himself into the debt of scholars who have passed this way before. The work which Professor Thomas A. Schafer, of McCormick Theological Seminary, has done with the *Miscellanies* is especially indispensible. All quotations from that rich source are taken from Dr. Schafer's typescript copy, with his permission and with the permission of the Beinecke Rare Book and Manuscript Library of Yale University whose staff has been most generous in its help.

I cannot omit my gratitude to Professor Sydney Ahlstrom of Yale University, who first introduced me to Edwards, and to Professor Gordon Harland of Drew University, whose vigorous criticism of several of the arguments in this book gave considerable stimulation to the entire effort.

There are words of darkness that must fall upon this page: much of the material in this volume was written in anticipation of the late Professor Carl Michalson's intelligent and searching reading. Thoughts of his untimely death in a plane crash have left their mark on my interpretation of the subject matter of Jonathan Edwards' extraordinary life.

I should remind myself publicly that for all the mental delight and ache of writing, this book really lies in the background, and not in the foreground, of the main business of my life. My wife Alice and our three children, Lisa, Keene, and Jamie, have never allowed love to be an idea. I have learned far more from them than from Jonathan Edwards.

JAMES CARSE

Washington Square, Autumn, 1967

CONTENTS

7

PROLOGUE

In his great painting of the nativity the fifteenth century artist, whom we know only as the Master of Flemalle, brought into his subject matter an astonishing contemporaneity. Joseph and Mary, the attending midwives, and the adoring shepherds are conspicuously clothed in the highest style of the time. Behind the nativity scene a stylized Flemish countryside reaches back an infinite distance into the rich golden light of a new age. The work has about it a casual, quiet, pleasant air, in spite of the abundance of detail. We sense that the figures were friends of the artist, perhaps his students or his relatives, urged patiently to hold their pose until he could by means of his art translate them into the eternity of two-dimensional space. They seem unconcerned with the infant Christ who lies naked on the open ground, like a child's discarded doll. The manger appears to be a hastily constructed prop, to be dismantled by the artist when his work is finished.

Five centuries removed, the subject matter of the painting is all but lost. Only the title and a few traditional symbols save us from thinking that the artist was merely executing portraits of miscellaneous personages otherwise forgotten by history. Our eye is attracted to the curious clothes or the tiny angels floating motionlessly over the scene, and languidly we wonder what moved the painter to undertake the work. It is a piece for a museum, something to be studied with the help of a guide book, or a professor. But how stunning this portrait must have been to the contemporary viewer. For where else would he have found the visual image of his Lord? Only in the crude graffiti of priests drawn for the enlightenment of dull and restless catechumens, or in the dark crucifixes that stared down upon them with Gothic awesomeness in the churches and cathedrals. This was an age in which no works of art were reproduced, in which the eye was not exhausted by the commercial exploitation of color on the printed page. To behold a great painting was an experience infrequent and therefore memorable in a man's life. Thus, all the more memorable was this Christ child and this holy family of their own flesh and blood, radiant and waiting under the plenitude of the Flemish sun.

The Master of Flemalle was a very great artist not because he could execute a precise likeness of contemporary styles, but because he could powerfully communicate a subject matter that had to do with the very life and health of the souls of his fellow supplicants. The Master of Flemalle was not concerned simply to reproduce an event that had once occurred in history past and then never again. Rather, it was the art of the painter to establish the meaning of that moment in history for the present age. He was a great artist because he knew his was a subject matter that could not be stated on a title-plate nor frozen in the sterile memory of a museum. The Christ of the Master of Flemalle was not the mechanically stiff infant lying at the feet of his models, but he was the Christ whose birth is the effulgence of light into a world that once was dark. In his Christ there was order and peace, the promise of an infinite future. To have painted the Christ child "as he was in fact" would have communicated none of this.

But then has anyone ever painted Christ as he was in historical fact? Indeed, has any subject ever been so painted? Were Rembrandt's self-portraits the "real" Rembrandt? Who was the real Rembrandt anyway? Was the real Rembrandt the dark image of himself which the artist beheld in the glass of his turbulent soul, or was he the man the butcher knew, or the neighborhood children? We are wont to talk with great confidence about "historical fact" as though a person or an event were a *res in facto posita,* an unchanging thing over which the stream of time has passed with no other effect than extending the distance of the viewer. But any man who goes seriously to the task of executing a portrait or a history soon learns that if there are real persons behind the appearances, behind the words and actions of visible men and events, we do not have the luxury of knowing them. What is certain is that when we do suppose we know the real person then we have frozen him into a fixed conception, we have made him a lifeless object, we have represented him as in a death out of which nothing new can come. Therefore, we shall never have the real Christ; we shall have only the words of the Christ-tellers, and only the voices of the Christ-singers. Nor shall we have the real Caesar, or the real Kennedy; we shall have only their chroniclers and their poets.

The very possibility of portraiture and history is in itself witness to the fact that each man is another's poet. The history of a human life is only what is spoken by others, either in their words or in their lives. Should a man be forgotten, should there be nothing to mark his passing, should there be no lives which sing his life, he has no history. He might not have lived at all. Each of us lives that others might know us, that others might translate us into the eternity of a told tale. Therefore each man is himself the portrait of the lives which have become history for him. His life is praise for that which he continues and urges others to take up with him; it is con-demnation of that which is not worth doing again. If por-traiture is life, life is portraiture.

What follows in these pages is a portrait of Jonathan Ed-wards. I begin with the knowledge that there is, after all, no such thing as the real Edwards. We might be momentarily deceived by the fact that Edwards did leave us some 20,000 pages of very real writing. There are scholars who believe that whatever might be said about Edwards it will be "true" or at least "reliable" if it comes from these pages. While hundreds of Edwards' actual words will be re-said in this portrait, we may not forget that his words too are portraiture. Edwards was a singer, a poet of things past. He was a gifted maker of the histories of others. In his life and in his pages are made visible a long tradition and a whole age. The subject matter of his works was depicted by means of doctrine, but it is no more equivalent to those doctrines than is the subject matter of the Master of Flemalle's painting stated on the brass title-plate. There is no going back to Edwards as though he were a *res in facto posita* over which time has passed without effect. My design in these pages is to bring Edwards as far forward as I can. We shall not be satisfied simply to sing the same words he had sung, nor shall we content ourselves with a slavish copy of the very marks he put upon his canvasses. We shall instead try to take up his subject matter and sing it anew.

Thus shall I paint Edwards—against a familiar but abstracted intellectual background. I shall ask him patiently to endure my labors until I can translate him into the idiom of an age strange to his. I shall drape him with the familiar habiliments of contemporary intellectual fashions, constructing around him a temporary academic framework of my own choosing. There is no intention in this to deceive. I hide nothing, as the Master of Flemalle hid nothing. For anyone knowledgeable of academic fashions my philosophic preferences are baldly apparent; for those ignorant of them, it is tiresome and unedifying to make them apparent.

I cannot pretend that others have not done this before me; Edwards has had his soldiers. In the first half-century after his death he was stuffed, armed, and mechanized by men who were certain that the whole crimson lava of truth was still sheltered under the granite of Calvinist dogma. And Edwards has had his spoilers. When the gentler breezes of the transcendentalist esthetes and the first luxuries of industrialism softened the academy, A. V. G. Allen guaranteed himself a place in the better libraries by crying "villain" over his portrait of a harshly insensitive Edwards. He has also had his professional chroniclers. "Amazing child prodigy," "last of the Puritans," "wilderness idealist," they have written in their anthologies and journals. And he has had his poets. From the bright labors of Perry Miller has come a monument of great beauty that will long stand. But in the pages that follow I shall use no space to argue with these and the many others who have come this way before; for I have no patience for museumship.

I have not come to teach my song, but to teach the hero I sing. And why is he a hero? He is a hero because the subject matter of which his life is a portrait has profoundly to do with the making of history two centuries down from his death.

I

THE MAN: TAPROOT
AND LEAF

$\mathcal{E}$very attempt to interpret the life or the thought of Jonathan Edwards must begin with the fact that he was an American. This is by no means an easy place to begin, for when we use the word "American" to describe Jonathan Edwards we must use it with all the ironic convergence of vision and fact, with all the vulgar urgencies and sophisticated energies of a remarkably durable and self-contradictory culture. No man will ever utter that final description of America; nor will anyone ever set to paper those words that exhaust the mystery of the turbulent genius of Jonathan Edwards. This much is certain: the one belongs to the other; the mystery of the one is the mystery of the other. It is here that we must begin.

Jonathan Edwards was an American because for almost a century before his birth in 1703 scores of ships had set upon the continent men and women whose uncommon ambitions, whether base or noble, had joined their destinies in the making of a new civilization. At first no one thought they were building anew. The tools of statecraft, the persuasions of religion, and the values of culture by which the people began to establish themselves were taken from an old civilization. Their vision was daring but it was not radical, for they wanted only the perfection of the old. They thought that by the just laws of an already ancient nation, and by its purified faith, they could build without blemish in a new place.

Nowhere can we see this more clearly than in the sermon John Winthrop delivered to his fellow voyagers in 1630 aboard the *Arrabella* somewhere "on the Attlantick Ocean." As the sea boiled around the bow of the ship, and the sails, set hard against the prevailing west wind, drove them steadily into the unknown, Winthrop spoke of "the worke wee haue in hand," which, as none needed to be reminded, was "to seeke out a place of Cohabitation and Consorteship vnder a due forme of Government both ciuill and ecclesiasticall."[1] But, for the most part, Winthrop's view was still over the stern of the *Arrabella*. If it was God's errand they were upon, then it was an errand in behalf of the godless England they had left behind. They were to be a "modell" society. Their task was not merely to build, he exhorted them, but to build a "Citty vpon a Hill," and may they never forget that the "eies of all people are vppon us."[2]

It is a significant clue to the mystery of the American soul, and the soul of Jonathan Edwards, that when Winthrop did look ahead, when he did give shape to that experience that lay before them, it was not a democratic parliamentary government, or the refinements of modern civilization that informed his thinking, but the sentences of holy scripture. As they sat there on the *Arrabella* with the chill salt spray in their faces and the universe in their hands, Winthrop cried out that the only way they would avoid the "shipwracke" of God's wrath in this great venture

is to followe the Counsell of Micah, to doe Justly, to loue mercy, to walke humbly with our God, for this end, wee

---

[1] "A Modell of Christian Charity," *The Puritans*, ed. Perry Miller and Thomas H. Johnson (New York, 1963), I, 197.   [2] *Ibid.*, I, 199.

must be knitt together in this worke as one man, wee must entertaine each other in brotherly Affeccion, wee must be willing to abridge our selues of our superfluities, for the supply of others necessities, wee must vphold a familiar Commerce together in all meekenes, gentlenes, patience and liberallity, wee must delight in eache other, make others Condicions our owne, reioyce together, mourne together, labour, and suffer together, allwayes haueing before our eyes our Commission and Community in the worke, our Community as members of the same body, soe shall wee keepe the vnitie of the spirit in the bond of peace . . .[3]

Jonathan Edwards was an American because the England that John Winthrop left behind never chose to follow. He was an American because the children and grandchildren of those who heard Winthrop's words above the yielding waters of the "Attlantick" no longer wanted to look backwards, neither to England nor to the prophet Micah. By the middle of Winthrop's century, either by the grace of God or by the confluence of a good climate, rich natural resources, and willing hands, the young Americans had raised their city upon a hill. But increasingly the eyes that fell upon that hill did not see there a refuge for an embattled faith as much as they saw in its prosperity the promise of fortune. Those who now disembarked on the oaken wharves of the American harbor cities were not pilgrims as much as they were refugees; they were not visionaries as much as they were adventurers. Indeed, there were some Americans landing on the continent in that century who by their presence alone tell us more about that early civilization than all our sentimentalized histories have been able to conceal: these were the Americans who had been seized out of a primitive society, who were strong enough to survive a sea voyage of twenty weeks or more in the airless heat of a ship's hold, bound by chain and manacle to their own vomit

[3] *Ibid.,* I, 198.

and defecation and terror, only to be sold to other Americans for coin. What Winthrop saw over the bow of the *Arrabella* with his fellow voyagers was a holy commonwealth; what they built was a thriving Nineveh.

Jonathan Edwards was an American because by the time he was born the old traditions and institutions which had come with the people now belonged to the land. They had been transformed by the land. The laws were English, but the lawbreakers were American. The concept of justice and the desire for an ordered society remained the same, but criminality had to be reinterpreted in light of the peculiar importance of one man to another in the new society. Adultery was punishable by death, but the wilderness town could not afford to lose the eighteen hours of hard work a healthy woman could give each day.

As the laws were English, the faith was Puritan, but the land was transforming that as well; for now there was neither prince nor prelate by whose persecution dogma could become witness. When the Puritan preacher in politically volatile England made public expression of his faith, the threatened loss of his tongue or his ears, or even his life, gave his words a special incandescence; and for his courage he was rewarded the fanatical loyalty of a congregation. But the repetition of those same words in economically stable New England was threatened only with an empty church. The passionate sentences with which the English Puritans chronicled their external warfare with the principalities of the world, and their internal embrace of the Spirit of God, seemed awkward and excessive in the new society. They required a greater exactitude of private and social morality, and a more powerful hegemony of the church, than seemed necessary to guarantee the increase of a prosperity wrought by hands alone.

In his history of the church in the first American century,

Cotton Mather makes reference to this transformation of the old religion in the new world with his poignant lament that though there were "preserving and prosperous smiles from heaven upon them," it was only a few short decades before "people began notoriously to forget the *errand into the wilderness,* and . . . to neglect the primitive designs and interests of *religion* propounded by their fathers."[4] When preachers called men before God according to the religion propounded by their fathers, they lost the attention of their sons, because they now had their eyes on the profane and fascinating hill that had become America.

Jonathan Edwards was an American because for three generations his family had lived out their busy lives on the new continent. The story of his family, in fact, closely parallels that of America itself. The first Edwards to take sail from England, his great-grandfather William, came with a stepfather whose mind was filled with the inflammatory credo of a Dissenter's faith, but whose motive for the journey, more appropriately, was the certainty of imprisonment for indebtedness had he remained. Edwards' paternal grandfather, Richard, was the first to be born on American soil, and for most of his seventy-one years was a prominent citizen of Hartford. Edwards' father, Timothy, was the long and faithful, if not brilliant, minister of the Connecticut River parish of East Windsor. The only one of Edwards' forbears to have achieved genuine fame was his maternal grandfather, the redoubtable Solomon Stoddard, pastor of the church in Northampton and initiator of the final debate over the Half-Way Covenant in which he proved the David, and Boston's Increase Mather the Goliath.

Jonathan Edwards was an American because, like his grandfather Richard, the chief struggle of his life was the attempt

[4] *Magnalia Christi Americana* (2 vols.; Hartford, 1820), II, 270.

to establish and sustain a style of living that would prosper in the present time and place. However faithful he may have seemed at times to "the primitive designs and interests" of that religion propounded by his fathers, Edwards never understood himself or his civilization to be embarked on an errand at the behest of another people. The "Citty vpon a Hill" was for Edwards a given, it was the fact from which he began. Richard Edwards and his contemporaries had built well, and Jonathan never rued their accomplishments. He never turned, like a Jeremiah blazing with the memory of a righteous past, to condemn the very foundations of his society. This had been the style of preachers a half-century before him, men whose religious sensibilities made it impossible for them to see that the American present was anything but a violation of their sacred Puritan inheritance. Like men awakened in a strange place, they preferred the dream to the cold, clear light of a new dawn. Edwards steadfastly refused to address his contemporaries from the imagined glory and lofty irrelevance of another era. He was a man of the present age. His prophetic voice was contemporary. Behind all his preachments we can still hear the stirring "Now!" that electrified his congregations.

By no means, however, may we say that Edwards was making a simple affirmation of the present at the expense of the past. On the contrary, it was because he was keenly sensitive to what had already transpired in man's journey across this earth that he was so alive to the present. Here we come to another feature in the make-up of Jonathan Edwards' life, a feature that gives still more subtlety to the fact that he was an American. Jonathan Edwards was the son of his father. Whatever other distinctions may not have come to Timothy Edwards in his lifetime, he did succeed in nourishing his precocious son's mind with the pure, but inelegant, broth of Calvinism. The precise importance of this fact in Edwards' life and thought is difficult properly to assess. We could pass over it with haste and say without elaboration that "Edwards must be regarded as the most eminent of American Calvinists,"[5] or we could bitterly regret it and cry out with one of his nineteenth century interpreters, "Edwards! What a career had been his, what discoveries had he made, if he had obeyed God instead of Calvin!"[6] Or, eschewing speculation as to how far one could follow both God and Calvin, we could recognize that what Edwards learned from the Calvinist tradition was, above all else, an overwhelming sense that history was but the unfolding of God's eternal design. Every happening in the experience of man is properly understood only when we can perceive its place in the economy of the great divine work of redemption. As the young Jonathan seized onto this conception he came to two conclusions that count heavily in the subsequent development of his thought. First, he thought there would appear in the normal course of human history, but as a prelude to its end, a period of several thousand years in which the forces of evil would have been crushed, allowing man to live out his earthly years in the enjoyment of every human blessing.

Secondly, he became convinced that the American civilization would play a major role in the piece of history that lay between the present and the coming millennium. In the year 1742, at the latter end of the Great Awakening, Edwards wrote *Some Thoughts Concerning the Present Revival of Religion in New England,* in which he allowed that the late and dramatic appearance of the Spirit in the lives of his fellow Americans had led him to think that the New Jerusalem "has begun to come down from heaven, and perhaps never were more of the prelibations of heaven's glory given upon earth."[7] Awk-

---

5 John T. McNeill, *The History and Character of Calvinism* (New York, 1954), p. 362.

6 Mattoon M. Curtis, "Kantian Elements in Jonathan Edwards" pamphlet (Berlin: 1906).

7 *The Works of President Edwards,* a reprint of the Worcester Edition, 4 vols. (New York: Jonathan Leavitt and John F. Trow, 1843), III, 309. Hereafter any citation for *Works* will refer to this edition unless otherwise stated.

wardly concealing the excitement he must have felt with this expectation, he then commented dryly, "It is not unlikely that this work of God's Spirit, that is so extraordinary and wonderful, is the dawning, or at least, a prelude of that glorious work of God, so often foretold in Scripture, which in the progress and issue of it shall renew the world of mankind."[8] That the renewal of mankind, and the establishment of the Kingdom of Christ, should begin in America seemed plain to Edwards. In fact, he thought the new world was discovered in order that "the new and most glorious state of God's church on earth might commence there; that God might in it begin a new world in a spiritual respect, when he creates the *new heavens* and *new earth*."[9] "So that as soon as this new world is (as it were) created, and stands forth in view, God presently goes about doing some great thing to make way for the introduction of the church's latter day glory, that is to have its first seat in, and is to take its rise from that new world." Perhaps overreaching himself, he reasons that if "this glorious work of God shall begin in any part of America, I think if we consider the circumstances of the settlement of New England, it must need appear the most likely of all American colonies, to be the place whence this work shall principally take its rise."[10]

Elsewhere Edwards indicates that what is about to happen in America will soon spread to all the world. "The changing of the course of trade and the supplying of the world with its treasures from America," he wrote into his private notes, "is a type and forerunner of what is approaching in spiritual things, when the world shall be supplied with spiritual treasures from America."[11] It is a short step from here to the conviction that America is the vanguard in God's warfare with

8 *Works*, III, 313.   9 *Works*, III, 314.   10 *Works*, III, 315.
11 *Images or Shadows of Divine Things*, ed. Perry Miller (New Haven, 1948), No. 147, p. 102.

the forces of darkness in this world, not only the place where the kingdom will begin but also an agent in its establishment.

Because he was born and educated into the Calvinist intelligibility, Edwards did not regard the past as something to which we must return, nor could he regard the present as something with which we are to be satisfied. Both the past and the present for Edwards are but preparation for the future. God brought us to this place across the sea, he brought us out of the "rotting" culture of England, in order to establish something new. Edwards is an American, therefore, not merely by virtue of his past, but also because he had a strong and clear vision of the future. Edwards is like John Winthrop, still looking back over the stern, ever aware of that which lies behind in the experience of history. But also like Winthrop he is brave enough to take out of the past whatever is worth saving and, throwing himself along with his intellectual heritage onto the mercy of the winds of history, he is determined to drive on into the unknown for the sake of coming ever closer to the ultimate society.

There is, however, an important difference between the two men; Edwards was an American in the way in which Winthrop was not. Between the two there lay a century, a hundred years in which the viability of Winthrop's vision could be tested. Because he could look back over the century Edwards had a much more complete understanding of the proclivities of the human heart for the duller stuff of physical comfort and security. He knew much more vividly than Winthrop how the articles of a living faith can be metamorphosed into dogmas of ownership and privilege. What Winthrop could never have imagined was now a fact for Edwards: when the *Arrabella* was moored in Boston harbor it was not the end of a journey but the beginning of one still more treacherous.

This knowledge would have been academic for Edwards had it not been for something even more significant in his life. He was the grandson of Solomon Stoddard. Perhaps there was no person in Edwards' view who could have more dramatically and completely evidenced the irony that lay at the center of the American experience. The narrative of Stoddard's affairs begins with that withering of religious passions that set upon the American people somewhere in the third or fourth decade of their "Plantation." When the ringing exhortations of their preachers failed to reverse the rapid secularization of society, it became apparent that the church would not long survive, for now it was scarcely more than the possession of a handful of old people who were waiting patiently to take it into the grave with them. It was the famous Synod of 1662 that managed finally to work a compromise between the spiritual rigor of the past and the fecklessness of the present. Ecclesiastically, the dilemma was focused on what had been to that time a major conviction of Puritanism: the church of Christ was to be composed of those who not only could *profess* their regeneration, but could also manifest *visible signs* of it to the charitable judgment of the congregation. As time went on this put outside the circle the increasing number of those who had no experience of regeneration to profess. There was the added loss to the church of the children of the unregenerate, since the failure of their parent's spirit to respond to the divine influences made it illegal for them to be baptized. The Synod's compromise, appropriately called the Half-Way Covenant by its opponents, allowed those who could give no evidence of conversion to have a restricted membership. They could have their children baptized, but they could not receive communion.[12]

But compromise is not solution, and especially not when the proposed compromise is itself inconsistent. Despite the vigorous support of the Synod's articles by New England's

[12] Cf., Williston Walker, *The Creeds and Platforms of Congregationalism* (New York, Charles Scribner's Sons, 1893), I. 313ff.

most eminent divines, the Half-Way Covenant did not rescue the church from its continuing ill fortune. At the turn of the century Solomon Stoddard took it upon himself to make the crooked places straight. In the year 1707, from his pulpit in Northampton, he delivered a sermon whose title alone was a call to arms: "The Inexcusableness of Neglecting the Worship of God under a Pretence of Being in an Unconverted Condition." The laws prescribed for worship and participation in the public acts of the church were no longer to be understood as exclusive of those who could not profess "experimental"[13] piety. The sacraments, he said, are not to be understood as a professing ordinance, but as a converting ordinance. "God in the Lord's Supper invites us to come to Christ, makes an affecting representation of his suffering for our sins."[14] Increase Mather accused Stoddard of requiring unsanctified persons to come to the table; and Stoddard replied that the accusation "is not fairly laid down, my position is, That Sanctifying Grace is not necessary to the lawful attending the Ordinance of the Lord's Supper."[15] Stoddard's theological defense of this position is essentially that unconverted souls should not be restricted from the table on *that* ground, because it is conversion above all else that is not in their power. It appeared to most observers and participants in this debate that both reason and good sense were on Stoddard's side, and eventually "he carried most of New England with him."[16] But the judgment of history is different. By this move, Miller tells us, Stoddard

> took into the communion not merely the professing adults,
> but all adults. At one fell swoop he cured the evils of the

[13] The Puritan equivalent for "experiential."

[14] Quoted by Frank Hugh Foster, *A Genetic History of the New England Theology* (Chicago, 1907), p. 39.

[15] *A Guide to Christ, or, the Way of Directing Souls that are under the Work of Conversion* (Cornhill, 1714), p. 2.

[16] Ola Winslow, *Jonathan Edwards 1703–1758* (New York, 1961), p. 103.

Half-Way Covenant by going beyond it; he uprooted the New England Way in Northampton, and identified the visible church no longer with the community of saints, but with the town meeting—where he himself was dictator and lawgiver.[17]

In 1727 Edwards left his briefly-held teaching post at Yale to serve as an assistant to his aging but still powerful grandfather. Even though there were but two years remaining in Stoddard's life Edwards had come so far under his spell that it would be almost fifteen years before he would see the damage that had been done by that seeming victory in the Half-Way Covenant debate. Most references to Jonathan Edwards in American historical literature isolate his prominent role in the Great Awakening as that which deserves most to be remembered. This is far from the truth. Without any doubt the most significant event in Edwards' life was his brave decision to contravene his grandfather on the question of visible sainthood. Scarcely anyone in his day, and scarcely anyone in ours, will celebrate him for this. It would appear to most judgments as a thinly-veiled attempt to reestablish the arbitrary tyranny of dogma over consciences made free by the Reformation. It would so appear, that is, to anyone who cannot understand that when Edwards stood out alone against his congregation and against the popular memory of Solomon Stoddard he was bringing to full expression the fact that he was an American.

Solomon Stoddard had won for churchmen and townsmen alike the privilege of a private faith, the right to make one's own commerce with God a matter that concerned no other person. Stoddard could appeal to his partisans on grounds they all considered valid: no man has access to another's soul. But Edwards saw it differently. He had learned from his ex-

[17] "Solomon Stoddard, 1643–1729," *Harvard Theological Review*, XXXIV (1941), p. 298.

perience as shepherd of the Northampton souls that no man can for long conceal the true inclinations of his heart. If there be wickedness in it, no external appearance can long mask it; nor will the charitable eye fail to see in the lives of true saints the signs of genuine gracious affections. Edwards knew that because the church had capitulated to the world, it could do nothing more than apply the stamp of its vapid, pious approval to whatever the world wanted to do. The church had ceased to act as a moral influence in the very society which its moral courage had created.

This violated what Edwards thought was the peculiar character both of America and the Christian faith because it reduced all talk about the ultimate society to harmless babble. America was no longer under the leadership of daring captains; it had submitted itself to helmsmen satisfied to sail free before the winds of their immediate prosperity without ever considering whither their course might take them. The Americans of Stoddard's generation forgot they had a history. As a result they saw nothing in the future but an indefinite extension of the present.

It is essential to this chronicle to understand that when Edwards revived the doctrine and the principle of visible sainthood, he was not doing so merely as a zealous critic of his own age. This was a theological decision as much as it was an ecclesiastical and political decision. As we shall see, the concept of visibility runs straight through the whole of Edwards' thought. It is the thesis of this book that when we understand what Edwards has comprehended under the term "visibility" we shall have located the vital center of his thought. For Solomon Stoddard, and for nearly all Americans after him, the chief characteristic of religious faith and all things divine was their *invisibility*. The story of Edwards' life, both as a thinker and as a shepherd of souls, is the story of his refusal to accede to the principle of private judgment in matters of religious and ethical importance. The pain and disorder which this refusal brought into Edwards' life make it obvious that his thinking about the nature of visibility was by no means casually developed, nor was it lightly held. He could never have separated his commitment to the principle of visibility from the fact that he was an American and a Christian.

While it is the principle of visibility that gives Edwards' thought its sharpest profile over against the Christian theological tradition, we should have erred if we think he intended to enunciate a novel doctrine. Edwards was giving expression to what he thought was most valid in the theological tradition as he had received it. With uncanny brilliance he brought all that was most valuable out of the Christian past before his view, and caused it to focus on the question of how one is to live as a Christian and as an American within the dimensions of his own time and place. It is here that we come closest to the greatness of Jonathan Edwards, for here in the clarity of his perception the genius of the Christian faith and the genius of America were caused to embrace each other in a single intense moment. Edwards' understanding of America was a Christian understanding. He saw America as a new event in God's establishment of universal peace and justice. At the same time, his understanding of the Christian faith was an American understanding. He selected from the Christian tradition those themes which had to do with the building of the promised society in an empty wilderness.

The immediate outcome which Edwards' reinstatement of this old Puritan principle excited in his church should not have caused surprise. As he rigorously pushed his congregation toward a decision, it was the minister and not the issue against which they finally acted. Jonathan Edwards, by the vote of an overwhelming majority of his church, was relieved of his ministerial duties. This was the year 1750. He was then at the

summit of his intellectual powers. A half-dozen more volumes
were to come from his pen, including the massive and virtuosic
Freedom of the Will, and he would serve without bitterness
the Indian mission in Stockbridge. The last few weeks of his
life would be honored with the dignity of the presidency of
Princeton College. But the decision of his congregation in
1750 is an event that must stand like a sentinel over all that
is to be said or written about Jonathan Edwards. For in terms
that mattered most to him he was a failure.

It is, for these reasons, a serious mistake on the part of the
interpreters of Jonathan Edwards to see him as simply another
Calvinist, a European intelligence flourishing a brief moment
on foreign soil. It is also a mistake to see him as the last of
the great Puritans, borne by his uncommon ability to grasp
and restate the *élan* of the most dynamic spiritual movement
since the Reformation. Nor may we see him as a philosophical
genius rising inexplicably out of the crude illiteracy of an
unmannered society, spinning out his heady idealism before
the stony countenances of plowboys and dark-skinned natives.
Seen in any of these ways, Edwards' image for his interpreters
becomes that of the misunderstood genius, separated by a
century or by an ocean from those who were truly able to
appreciate his mental fecundity. By such a view of the man and
his background we can interpret him only as a tragedy.

This book intends squarely to overturn such an interpretation of Jonathan Edwards. Because he was so fully an American and so alert to the ambiguities of the American civilization,
we cannot understand him as a tragedy. We can understand
him only as a failure. To see him as tragic, as a misunderstood
genius, is to fail to see the greatness of the man; it is to fail
to see how important the story of his life and thought is to
every American age. To regard Edwards as tragic is to
suppose that the relocation of his thought will repair the
damage done to the man's reputation, if not to the man him-

self. We could put him in the idealist tradition, or group him with the Calvinists, or anthologize him with John Bunyan and John Milton. Then his awkwardness as an American disappears. But so does the man disappear, because Edwards was not as great a philosopher as Berkeley, nor were his dogmatic systems as detailed and thorough as Beza's or Turretini's, nor does his imagination glisten with the allegoric swiftness of the great Puritan poets. Such an interpretation of Edwards is not only idle scholarship; it is to look at, without seeing, the one moment in which the ironies of American history and the paradoxes of the Christian faith merge and become one.

II

MR. LOCKE'S MAGIC
ONIONS AND AN
UNBOXED BEETLE FOR
YOUNG JONATHAN

*T*he queerness of Jonathan Edwards' youth creates a special
but attractive problem for the interpreter of this thought.
So intellectually precocious was this child of the American wilderness that he managed to telescope what is for most
intelligent men an entire lifetime of mature reflection into
the few years of his adolescence. By the time he had begun
the serious theological work of his adulthood he had developed a highly refined point of view and a peculiarly lucid self-
understanding of his vocation as pastor and theologian. It is
more truly said of Jonathan Edwards than almost any other
great mind that we cannot know the man until we have
known the boy.

Where other children use their daydreams to transport
themselves into adventures of exotic delight or into the heroic
mastery of danger, young Edwards sent his in pursuit of the
truth that always seemed to lie just beyond the edge of dark
adult puzzlements. The world around him, alive and rushing

with a million discoverable things, pointed to secret facts which he thought the world itself could not contain. As he watched the spiders in the field behind his house aloft on their "little shining webbs and Glistening Strings of a Great Length and at such a height as that one would think they were tack'd to the Sky by one end were it not that they were moving and floating,"[1] he wondered by what design it was that they should be swept up at the end of the summer and blown out to sea. When the sugar maples showered their yellow leaves like a brilliant liquid in the October wind, his thoughts yielded not to poetry but to deep theories on the nature of color. Never out of sight of the black fist of infant mortality, much too frequent in the rural town, he felt constrained to speculate on the nature of the soul. The surging power of the Connecticut River in the spring so captured his imagination that years later, in his most famous sermon, he could let all its power rush forth in words.

> The wrath of God is like great waters that are dammed for the present; they increase more and more, and rise higher and higher, till an outlet is given; . . . If God should only withdraw his hand from the flood-gate, it would immediately fly open, and the fiery floods of the fierceness and wrath of God, would rush forth with inconceivable fury, and would come upon you with omnipotent power; and if your strength were ten thousand times greater than it is, yea, ten thousand times greater than the strength of the stoutest, sturdiest devil in hell, it would be nothing to withstand or endure it.[2]

Other children let their imaginary extravagances disappear forever into a pleasant mindlessness, but the child Jonathan took pen to paper and there left a permanent record of the

[1] "Of Insects," *Jonathan Edwards,* ed. Clarence H. Faust and Thomas H. Johnson (New York, 1962), p. 3.
[2] "Sinners in the Hands of an Angry God," *Ibid.,* p. 163.

first tender fruits of his unfolding genius. There are several kinds of manuscripts in these writings. The earliest of which we have any knowledge is the essay on the flying spider, probably written during his eleventh year. There is a brief disquisition on the nature of being, and several others on the rainbow, the soul, and science. The most interesting manuscript, and the one most useful to us, Edwards himself titled "Notes on the Mind." This accumulation of paragraphs on such subjects as beauty, truth, excellency, virtue, proportion, and harmony, seems to have come out of his years at Yale. They are frequently in response to what he has been reading, and most often in response to the philosopher John Locke.

These manuscripts are not easy to read. They are partial and miscellaneous. Sometimes he becomes impatient with an argument and moves on to another before he has finished with it. Sometimes he never seems to tire of a point, pausing to wander about it in repeated circles. But there are flashes of lightning, moments when his pen rushes suddenly ahead. Occasionally we have the sensation that we have watched him set down an idea at the very moment of its discovery.

Scholars of Edwards' writings and critics of his position have properly invested these youthful ruminations with great importance, but they have usually been careless in their interpretation of them. These pages have been read as though they were not formulated on the run, but as though they were put down only when the thought had been permanently fixed in its author's mind. The greater number of his readers have decided that "philosophical idealism" is the term most accurately descriptive of their content. In fact, speculation has not infrequently run to investigating how Edwards, before he was scarcely out of his childhood, could have come upon the works of Bishop Berkeley. It is simply incredible that a mere youth on the American frontier could not only have read the works of John Locke, but could also have executed a critique of Locke remarkably similar to Berkeley's. Undeniably, there are passages which seem to require such an interpretation. In the course of his inquiry into Locke's teaching on the nature of substance, he writes:

> And, indeed the secret lies here: That, which truly is the Substance of all Bodies, is *the infinitely exact, and precise, and perfectly stable Idea, in God's mind, together with his stable Will, that the same shall gradually be communicated to us, and to other minds, according to certain fixed and exact established Methods and Laws*: or in somewhat different language, *the infinitely exact and precise Divine Idea, together with an answerable, perfectly exact, precise and stable Will, with respect to correspondent communications to Created Minds, and effects on their Minds.*[3]

Admittedly there is something Berkeleyan in this passage —the notion that it is the idea in the mind of God that constitutes substance—but the case is unclear, for at the same time there is also ground for calling Edwards a "rationalist" in the sense that there are available to the mind categories of thought that are identical in their operation to categories in the divine mind and that, therefore, all knowledge can be excogitated. "Rationalism is not the whole of Edwards' philosophy," one of the students of these early writings argues, "but it is the basis of it."[4]

It is a curious and unfortunate fact that Edwards has been remembered by the chroniclers of American intellectual history more for the tentative and diffuse remarks of his youth than for the immense production of his mature years. What is never taken full account of is that nearly all of the properly philosophical material in the body of Edwards' work was

---

[3] *"The Mind" of Jonathan Edwards,* ed. Leon Howard (Berkeley, California, 1963), No. 13, p. 54.

[4] Harvey G. Townsend, *The Philosophy of Jonathan Edwards from his Private Notebooks* (Eugene, Oregon, 1955), pp. viiif.

written before his seventeenth year, and scarcely ever appears after that time either in his published writings or in his private miscellaneous reflections. After his senior year at Yale[5] we find that he almost never concerned himself with such problems as substance, truth, rules of reasoning, identity of person, number, duration, and being. Therefore, instead of looking for some sort of philosophical position in the early stages of its development, it would seem wiser to determine why he so abruptly ceased these avid philosophical inquiries.

In the writings of his adult years it was a striking, and sometimes annoying, characteristic of his intellectual labor that he tirelessly hunted down every implication and consequence of an argument until he had proved it either true or absurd. There is no reason to think he was not doing that as a boy in these early pages. It would appear that he was undertaking a vigorous assault on the best philosophical arguments his age could provide him. He pursued each as far as it could take him, then, when he had perceived whither he had gone with it, he abandoned it. Now we must find out why.

John Locke was the greatest philosopher to have been born to English soil since Duns Scotus. It is a piece of good fortune that his collected writings should have been at Edwards' hand while the boy's thoughts were abuilding. Locke was a comprehensive and moderate thinker. The great value of his philosophy was not so much the creativity or the novelty of his ideas as it was his ability to rework the historic themes of Western thought into his own distinctive system. Locke's

---

[5] I am following Leon Howard's suggestion that Edwards wrote the "Notes on the Mind" in his senior year, since "they are not only unconventional. They are rebellious. They attack the whole intellectual system of Yale, and, surprisingly enough in view of Edwards' later remarks about his youthful enthusiasm for Locke, they consistently attack his monumental *Essay*. They are the work of an astonishingly independent mind—a mind that might have had its independence bolstered by three years in a rebellious environment." *Op. cit.,* p. 8.

reasonable and non-speculative philosophy could have developed only out of the sophistication of an established insular aristocracy. Edwards' was a society in which the illusion about life's stability was more difficult to sustain, but he was still sufficiently in the luxury of a privileged youth that he could afford to listen to everything the great thinker had to say.

Near the center of Locke's thought is the proposition that the mind is furnished with a great number of "simple ideas conveyed in by the senses as they are found in external things."[6] Knowledge, therefore, consists "in the view the mind has of its own ideas." "The different clearness of our knowledge," he adds, "seems to me to lie in the different way of perception the mind has of the agreement or disagreement of any of its ideas."[7] *"Knowledge* then seems to me nothing but *the perception of the connexion of and agreement, or disagreement and repugnancy of any of our ideas."*[8]

Aware that, on the basis of these remarks, he will be accused of "building a castle in the air,"[9] Locke makes a significant move in his philosophy. He guarantees the connection of the ideas with existing things. There are three kinds of existences with which our ideas are connected: our own being, God, and then all other sensible things. Where it is *intuition* by which we have knowledge of ourselves, and *reason* by which we have knowledge about God, *sensation* is assigned the task of providing the "necessary connection" between ideas and things. Sensation is made necessary only because "the having the idea of anything in our mind, no more proves the existence of that thing, than the picture of a man evidences his being in the world, or the visions of a dream make thereby a true history."[10] Believing that sensation is a mental act separable from the idea we have of it, he can say that it "is there-

[6] *An Essay Concerning Human Understanding,* ed. Alexander Campbell Fraser (2 vols.; New York, 1959), II, xxiii, 1.
[7] *Ibid.,* IV, ii, 1.   [8] *Ibid.,* IV, i, 2.   [9] *Ibid.,* IV, iv, 1.
[10] *Ibid.,* IV, xi, 1.

fore the *actual receiving* of ideas from without that gives notice of the existence of other things."[11]

The term "actual receiving" reminds us that the whole of Locke's philosophy follows from his original presupposition that the mind is "as we say, white paper, void of all characters, without any ideas," and that what furnishes the mind with "an almost endless variety" of ideas is "EXPERIENCE."[12] Once this presupposition has been granted, one does not affirm a connection between ideas and things by appealing to a metaphysical judgment, but by reflecting on what actually happens in experience. "He that *sees* a fire, may, if he doubt whether it be anything more than a bare fancy, *feel* it too; and be convinced, by putting his hand in it."[13]

From this it follows that when we come to judge whether knowledge be true, Locke must first insist that "truth as well as knowledge may well come under the distinction of verbal and real;" the former being an agreement between ideas without regard to that which they stand for, and the latter being an agreement between ideas which "are such as we know are capable of having an existence in nature."[14] Therefore, with a concept of such importance as, say, "causation," Locke must use it as though its validity rested on a particular relation *both in the mind and in reality.*

Substances, in the Lockean philosophy, are therefore to be understood as something like magic onions, and the mind as a box in which the sensations of substances are collected like skins from the magic onions. The onions are magic because no matter how many skins are removed they remain the same— and only the outer skin can be removed. Knowledge, according to this metaphor, can be but the variety of the arrangements of the skins in the box. If you ask what substances *really are* you cannot get an answer because all you can get of the magic

[11] *Ibid.,* IV, xi, 2.　　　[12] *Ibid.,* II, i, 2.　　　[13] *Ibid.,* IV, ii, 7.
[14] *Ibid.,* IV, v, 8.

onions are their skins. There is no amount of sense data that can give us the basis for judging what the onion really is because we can never see or feel more than the outside skin. Is experience then really capable of proving that there are real onions under the skins, or real substances under the sense data? It was with this question that Edwards began to draw Locke's conclusions into doubt.

Edwards assailed the philosopher's easy assumption that sensation points to the existence of the object which "occasions" the sensation. When we consider the idea of body, he says, it is color that has the chief share in it, but the idea also includes the powers of resisting and motion. Each of these, Edwards sees, is but another onion skin, another perception of the mind. "Colours are not really in the things, no more than pain is in a needle; but strictly nowhere else but in the mind." The same can be said of resistance: "What is it that is resisted? It is not Colour. And what else is it? It is ridiculous to say, that Resistance is resisted. . . . But now it is easy to conceive of Resistance, as a mode of an idea." The conclusion to this line of argument is inevitable: "This world is therefore an ideal one; and the Law of creating, and the succession of these ideas is constant and regular."[15]

Simply by pushing Locke's notion to a consistent conclusion, Edwards eliminates the externality of substance; but at the same time he has presented himself with a position that hangs on the edge of absurdity by its unashamed violation of common sense. However, characteristic of his mental tenacity, he will not stop even here. He will go on from the ideality of the world to the difficult notion that "Truth, in the general, may be defined, after the most strict and metaphysical manner, *The consistency and agreement of our ideas, with the ideas of God*."[16] Where Locke thought that truthfulness was related to agreement with reality, for Edwards it was with God. It is not far from here to the extreme, perhaps careless, remark that "God and real existence are the same."[17]

With what will prove to be a development significant throughout the remainder of his thought, Edwards indicates that he was himself aware of the danger in this seeming idealism. In perhaps the most important entry in these early manuscripts, he sees with perfect clarity that

> When we say that the World, i.e. the material Universe, exists no where but in the mind, we have got to such a degree of strictness and abstraction, that we must be exceedingly careful, that we do not confound and lose ourselves by misapprehension. That is impossible, that it should be meant, that all the world is contained in the narrow compass of a few inches of space, in little ideas in the place of the brain; for that would be a contradiction; for we are to remember that the human body, and the brain itself, exist only mentally, in the same sense that other things do and so that, which we call *place,* is an idea too. Therefore things are truly in those places; for what we mean, when we say so, is only, that this mode of our idea of place appertains to such an idea. We would not therefore be understood to deny, that things are where they seem to be. . . . Though we suppose, that the existence of the whole material Universe is absolutely dependent on Idea, yet we may speak in the old way, and as properly, and truly as ever.[18]

The implications of this early conclusion are so far-reaching, and so indicative of the modernity of Edwards' mind, that it is necessary to draw them out before we proceed. We must be careful first to hear precisely what he has said in this passage. Having argued that existence is itself an idea (as even Locke seems to have admitted[19]), he pushed ahead to the final

[17] *Ibid.,* No. 15, p. 101.   [18] *Ibid.,* No. 34, pp. 91f.
[19] Cf. *An Essay* (above, note 6) II, xxiii, 3.

consequence of this argument: the mind, too, is an idea. It was this logical conclusion to the starting point of his own philosophy that Locke never managed to attain. He could never rid himself of the metaphor of the mind as a container of ideas.

What is most important in this passage is not merely the rejection of Locke's position on the nature of existence; it is the boy's realization that "we may speak in the old way, and as properly, and truly as ever." These sentences of Edwards were not written for publication; they were but the record of his own thoughts set down for his own use. It is perhaps for this reason that he does not bother to expand on his phrase, "in the old way." We are left to fill in the meaning of this remark according to our own speculation, although we are not entirely without clues as to the direction it ought to take.

People who think and speak "in the old way" never deny, for one thing, "that things are where they seem to be." The reason for this is that they can probably *agree* that things are where they seem to be. In fact, almost never is anyone confused about this matter. Certainly there are instances when one has occasion to ask whether what he is looking at is an existing thing or merely an "appearing" thing. "Is that a person standing there in the dark, or is it a shadow?" But this is a question of small philosophic consequence, since it can be answered simply by shouting at the form, or throwing a stone at it. Normally, in ordinary discourse, the problem of the existence of things never arises, nor does it need to. No farmer in East Windsor would have paused to settle any doubts he might have had as to whether the stones forced up by the frost were real or ideal. They were just plain stones, as any fool could see.

When the young Edwards assured himself that he could speak in the old way, he was, in effect, opting for the notion that meanings are not private and individual, but public and conventional. The farmer can talk meaningfully about the stones in his pasture not because he has gone through the proper mental examination of the propositions concerning the existence of stones, but because his speaking about stones is a form of participating in a certain human community in which clearing fields in the spring and building fences is a common experience. Had the farmer begun talking about the ideas of stones which were in his head, he would surely have puzzled his friends.

Therefore, we can say that Edwards rejected Locke's notion of substance as something that existed somehow "behind," or in addition to, the perception of it, both because it was *false,* and because it was *unnecessary.* It was false because it rested on the validity of the magic onion metaphor; it was unnecessary because no one needed to raise the question of existence to proceed with the chief business of life. This does a great deal of damage to the Lockean philosophy. Edwards did not provide us with his view of the ruins in these notes, but we can see them for ourselves. Locke thought that those perceptions were accurate and those sentences true which were correctly related to the actual substances they named. Edwards saw that accuracy and truth had to do with what "appeared," not with what was "really there."

We must not pass over this point with too great haste since the term "appearance" will take on great importance in Edwards' later writings, and if we cannot determine now the precise way in which he is using the term we should be easily misled in our subsequent interpretation. In his famed inquiry into the freedom of the will, for example, he will rest his entire position on the statement that "the will is as the greatest apparent good is." And in his key essay on the satisfaction of Christ he will insist that the merit of Christ is an "apparent merit."

What should be clear in this early passage is that Edwards

is not drawing a metaphysical distinction between the "apparent" and the "real." When he decides that things are what they seem to be, or what they appear to be, he is not asserting that we are forever sundered from things as they "really are"; he is saying that appearances are all there are. To go behind appearances is to go to the inside of the magic onions, to enter into Locke's substances. This, he knew, was impossible both in thought and in experience.

Locke's supreme philosophic confidence suffered still another damaging blow in the young Edwards' private appraisal of it. Locke thought he could relate man to the world through the senses, and to himself through intuition, but when it came to God he decided that the relation could be built on *reason*. The position that Edwards has struck in these writings requires him to reject this as well. Like the Reformers two centuries earlier, he remained in fundamental mistrust of the capacity of reason to take one into the courts of the divine truth. But, unlike the Reformers, he stood on a philosophical, and not merely a religious, validity for this attitude toward reason. Once Edwards had seen that things are truly what they seem to be, and that we can now speak in the old way as properly and truly as ever, he knew that the task of reason was not to carry him beyond what the eyes can see and the ears can hear, because beyond what is visible there is nothing at all.

The task of reason, and its ancillary metaphysics, is to assist us in dealing with what we already know. While the scalpel of reason has rarely been applied more expertly than by the mature Edwards in his dissection of opponents' arguments, and while it may seem strange to that person who is familiar with the later imaginative explorations of the Northampton preacher into such secret places as the eternal fires of hell, we shall nonetheless claim that, consistent with these early pages, Edwards never gives in to the seductions of metaphysics. For he is not pretending to be able to make spiritual journeys into the deepest arcana of the divine mind; he is simply expanding on the "affectional" language of scripture that he might make an ever livelier appeal to the hearts of his listeners. On one occasion he does admit that " 'tis by metaphysical arguments only we are able to prove, that the rational soul is not corporeal; that lead or sand can't think; that thoughts are not square or round, or don't weigh a pound."[20] But more than this he will never let metaphysics do.

One might wonder, in this case, how it is possible for Edwards to talk about God at all. The question could be put this way: while it is perhaps clear what he means when he says that people are to talk about stones and other visible things "in the old way," can he also say they are to speak about God "in the old way"?

In the miscellaneous notes of a modern thinker there appears a picturesque illustration of this point, and one which might have amused a young philosophical observer of insects. We are asked to suppose that

> everyone had a box with something in it: we call it a "beetle." No one can look into anyone else's box, and everyone says he knows what a beetle is only by looking at *his* beetle.—Here it would be quite possible for everyone to have something different in his box. One might even imagine such a thing constantly changing.—But suppose the word "beetle" had a use in these people's language?— If so it would not be used as the name of a thing. The thing in the box has no place in the language-game at all; not even as a *something*: for the box might be empty.[21]

We already have the word "God," and while there is no direct acknowledgment of it in the "Notes on the Mind," it is evident that Edwards, either by design or by accident, has

---

[20] *Freedom of the Will*, ed. Paul Ramsey (New Haven, 1957), pp. 423f.
[21] Ludwig Wittgenstein, *Philosophical Investigations,* trans. G. E. M. Anscombe (New York, 1953), Para. 293, p. 100e.

worked himself into a clear-minded view of the usefulness of that word. If we can use the word "God" at all meaningfully, it is not because we have some private relationship with a distant being which no other person can see, but because there is some obvious basis of agreement for the use of the word within a certain human community. It is this understanding of the nature of religious language that provides the philosophical foundation for Edwards' application, during the latter years of his ministry in Northampton, of the old Puritan practice of judging the validity of a church member's profession by the visibility of his faith.

When Edwards was a boy he abandoned Locke's magic onions and resolved, like a man, to live in a world of unboxed beetles. Perhaps the reader will not yet be convinced that when the seventeen-year-old student wrote that "God and real existence are the same," he was not voicing a thoroughgoing idealism. But the life of the man, and the body of his mature thought, will secure the present judgment that these words are but an awkward attempt to state a radical thesis quite antithetical to idealism. He is saying that our relationship with God, and our knowledge of him, is made up out of the stuff of life. God comes to us not out of the sublime machinations of an unseeable and eternal universe, but out of the confused, unfinished histories of persons we know by name and sight and touch. From this point on, all of Edwards' talk about God had to do with the way men were to live with one another. He consistently refused to let God be put into an invisible box. Jonathan Edwards became the preacher of the visibility of God. For this reason he was great; for the same reason he was a failure.

III.

A CHAIN OF INFINITE
LINKS OR LIFE ITSELF?

*P*artly because he had already made himself known as a
preacher of considerable skill, but mostly because he
was now in command of Stoddard's controversial pulpit,
Edwards was invited to deliver the Public Lecture in Boston,
on July 8, 1731. This date should be well marked in our
chronicle of his intellectual passage. By this time he had lived
almost exactly half the number of years and days counted out
for him. Apart from the careful, doctrinal sermons delivered
during his first several years at Northampton there had been
no public access to his mind in the first half of his life. Unknown to any eye but his own were the hundreds of brief
essays and private reflections, neatly collected in his desk,
by which he had been putting together the inner machinery
of his thought. Now, in Boston, he would for the first time
bring a portion of this hidden conversation into the public
record. This sermon was to be Edwards' first published work.

If this was a significant moment in the life of Jonathan
Edwards, it was also a significant moment in the life of the
age. All previous alignments in American doctrinal and ecclesiastical history had become obscure. The clanking iron struc-
tures of Calvinism, kept dutifully in repair by Increase Mather

and the seventeenth century divines, could no longer serve to restrain the continuing decline of New England piety. What sparks were left of the once vivid fires of Puritanism had been stamped out by such modern men as Solomon Stoddard. Those who, in the midst of this religious lethargy, had allowed themselves to be convinced by Stoddard's sensible and human arguments, now could find no defense against Arminianism.[1]

What makes this moment propitious in the religious memory of America is that Edwards knew better than anyone else that he stood on the shifting sand of an age in transition. He knew that the past had to be quickly and accurately appraised so that the best could be saved out of it; but he also knew that a forceful, new application of it was necessary if the church was to prosper in the age being born. The miscellaneous notes, accumulating in his study, are proof that he had been reaching deep into the sand and that he believed that he had found the rock on which to build his intellectual battlements.

The sermon Edwards preached in Boston bore the title, *God Glorified in the Work of Redemption, by the Greatness of Man's Dependence on Him, in the Whole of it*. Insofar as the sermon was read, it was adjudged to be a sturdy Calvinist statement. It won for its writer the warm respect of the inner circle of orthodoxy. Not being able to see ahead into the second half of his life, as we can see it in retrospect, they failed to see that there was something new in his words. It is true that the sermon manfully embraces the doctrine of God's sovereignty, but it is not that which Edwards was chiefly expounding. It was not man's dependence but God's work of redemption that lay at the bottom of these sentences. He dis-

---

[1] In its narrower, doctrinal, sense the term "Arminian" is descriptive of the views of Jacob Arminius (1560–1609), a Dutch theologian who taught, contrary to the Calvinists then in theological ascendancy, that God's electing grace can be resisted. In its broader sense the term stands for a generally liberal attitude in religion, and for a confidence in human reason by no means shared by the "Calvinistick" or "Evangelical" party of which Edwards was a member.

cusses divine sovereignty only so far as it magnifies the greatness of that which God has given us; he does not intend by it
further to magnify the wretchedness of man. The reasons the
redeemed are so dependent on God are three: First, "all the
good that they have is in and through Christ."[2] Secondly,

> it is God that has given us Christ, that we might have these
> benefits through him. . . . Thirdly. It is of him that we
> are in Christ Jesus, and come to have an interest in him,
> and so do receive those blessings which he is made unto
> us. It is God that gives us faith whereby we close with
> Christ.[3]

It is not the doctrine of predestination, but the person of
Christ, that most decisively informs these first published words
of Jonathan Edwards.

What consequences are to come from this subtle but significant emendation of classical Calvinism are not immediately
evident in Edwards' life. The decade following the Boston lecture was the period of most conspicuous success in his ministry, but it was the kind of success that could have been vis-
ited on any able New England pastor. There is no question
that for Edwards personally these next ten years were the finest
in his life, but for our intellectual portrait there is little to
indicate in them what the final shape of his thought would
be. We only know that whatever that shape was to be, he intended the crisis and victories of the present moment to provide
him with the smithy for the swift hammers of his mind.

The first great personal victory came in the year 1735 when
his warm, evangelical preaching was rewarded with a vigorous
revival of religion in Northampton. The glory of this event
was brief, and it ended with tragedy,[4] but Edwards was filled

---

[2] *Works of President Edwards* (see Chap. one, footnote 7).

[3] *Works*, IV, 170.

[4] In a fit of melancholy set on by the revival, Joseph Hawley, a prominent
citizen in the town and Edwards' own uncle, cut his throat one Sunday
morning in the spring of 1735. Still other suicides were to follow.

with great expectations by it. A year after it was over he was still able to write to his friend Benjamin Colman of Boston rapturously describing this late appearance of the Spirit. Colman soon had this letter printed under the title, *A Faithful Narrative of the Surprising Work of God*. This was to become as famous during Edwards' lifetime as anything he would write.

In 1740, after a "dead" period in religion, the floodgates opened. A vast revival known as the Great Awakening suddenly carried away the greater part of New England. Edwards and his church were among the first to go. The efficient cause of the Awakening was George Whitefield, evangelist extraordinary, whose well-publicized arrival from England set off frenzied waves of religious zeal across the colony. Whitefield was cross-eyed and obese, and possessed of no great theological knowledge, but he could throw his great body about the pulpit with such abandon, and bellow out his histrionic clichés with such vocal power, that the vision of hell's torments danced before thousands in that full season of the Spirit.

Edwards had his own part in this strange chapter of American history. His preaching produced a number of masterpieces in the revivalist genre; and one of his sermons will forever mark him as a purveyor of severe maledictions. "Sinners in the Hands of an Angry God" was delivered in Enfield in the summer of 1741, for a congregation to whom Edwards was still a stranger. We are told that his preaching style was moderate in volume, and reverent in tone. He was not, like Whitefield and the scores of less subtle evangelists that modeled themselves after him, violent in the pulpit. For this sermon, and in this time, he need not have been. With language of immediate, homely clarity he explained to the anxious saints in Enfield that "Unconverted men walk over the pit of hell on a rotten covering, and there are innumerable places in this covering so weak that they will not bear their weight, and these places are not seen."[5] If any on that morning had looked for a word of comfort, some encouragement of hope, their preacher denied it to them.

> If you cry to God to pity you, he will be so far from pitying you in your doleful case, or showing you the least regard or favour, that instead of that, he will only tread you under foot. And though he will know that you cannot bear the weight of omnipotence treading upon you, yet he will not regard that, but he will crush you under his feet without mercy; he will crush out your blood, and make it fly, and it shall be sprinkled on his garments, so as to stain all his raiment.[6]

Perhaps surprisingly, it was not Edwards' preaching so much as it was his *Faithful Narrative* of the 1735 revival that contributed most effectively to the Great Awakening, for the little non-theological account of the conversion of particular persons in his congregation, written in a plain descriptive style, provided models for perfect regeneration, and thereby served as a sort of handbook for the Awakening. But there is considerable irony in this, because before the summer of 1741 was out the inevitable excesses of the widespread hysteria were beginning to appear, and Edwards was among the first leaders of the Awakening to see them. The revivals were coming increasingly under the control of shapeless passions. The most violent jerkings of the body and the loudest groans and screams were taken to be the truest signs of the presence of the Spirit. "As a result, the Great Awakening perished in its own noise."[7]

At the height of the revival Edwards wrote his *Distinguishing Marks of a Work of the Spirit of God,* obliquely disclosing

[5] Clarence H. Faust, and Thomas H. Johnson, eds. *Jonathan Edwards* (New York, 1902), p. 159.

[6] *Ibid.*, p. 167.

[7] Ola Elizabeth Winslow, *Jonathan Edwards 1703–1758* (New York, 1961), p. 183.

his alarm that in their zeal the people were losing all sense of
what is being wrought by the Spirit and what by the devil.
In 1742, the year following the Awakening, he delivered a
series of sermons in which he acknowledged that Satan had
indeed taken a prominent role in this affair. In his cooler reflection he noted how urgent it was that Christians be able
to tell gold from dross in religious experience. These sermons
were later published as the *Treatise on the Religious Affections*, a book certain to remain a classic in Christian literature.

The philosophical and theological conclusions at which Edwards had arrived more than ten years ago now caused him
to moderate his own role in the Awakening. He was still convinced that "True religion, in great part, consists in holy affections,"[8] but not any kind of affection would do. " 'Tis no sign
one way or the other," he wrote, "that religious affections are
very great, or raised very high."[9] Indeed, "there are religious
affections which are very high, that are not spiritual and saving."[10] Nor is it "a sign that affections have the nature of religion, or that they have not, that they have great effects on
the body."[11] Edwards was attacking the extremism of the
Awakening; he was not throwing it all away. When he had
rejected the more common standards for judging whether one
has truly gracious affections, he went on to provide signs
by which one could more reliably make this judgment. But
the twelve "positive" signs were too subtly composed for the
mood of the time. Violent passions are not moderated by
sober, philosophical rejoinders; they will either burn out and
leave ashes where there once was fire, or they will rage on un-
checked.

Apart from the handful of people who tried vainly to sustain the high excitement of the Awakening, Northampton was
returning to its normally secular style. Edwards' moderation

[8] *Religious Affections*, ed. John Smith (New Haven, 1959), p. 95.
[9] *Ibid.*, p. 127.   [10] *Ibid.*, p. 130.   [11] *Ibid.*, p. 131.

appealed to almost no one, and his earnest plea for balanced affections could scarcely be heard. The first decade of his ministry was over, and the second was begun much less auspiciously. There was soon a brief but bitter controversy over the amount of his salary, certain indication that the support of his congregation had lost must of its warmth. Evidence that his patience with his congregation had been exhausted is the incident he initiated by his public reprimand of a number of young persons caught reading a book on midwifery. His immoderate reaction to this affair betrays the frustration he must have felt at the moral torpor of the town so lately revived in matters of religion. Young Timothy Root was no doubt voicing the sentiment of many in Northampton when he said of the committee investigating his part in the affair that "They are nothing but men moulded up of a little Dirt; I don't Care a Turd, or I don't Care a Fart for any of them."[12]

It is in the latter part of this second decade of Edwards' ministry that we can see how important to his life was the private work of his mind. Apparently unimpressed with the precariousness of his position, he yielded to the desire to be consistent with himself and with the best of the Christian heritage as he knew it. *An Humble Inquiry into the Rules of the Word of God, Concerning the Qualifications Requisite to a Complete Standing and Full Communion in the Visible Christian Church,* published in 1749, was the book in which Edwards chose publicly to gainsay his grandfather. Stoddard had been dead more than twenty years, and while the charisma of his person was sustained in the memories of only a few, the results of his liberality had become fixed in the cultural habits of New England. If Edwards' eventual expulsion from the church in Northampton had ever been in doubt, the publication of this book guaranteed it.

For reasons not altogether clear Edwards chose, among the

12 Perry Miller, *Jonathan Edwards* (New York, 1959), p. 217.

several options open to him, to continue his ministry in the Indian mission post at Stockbridge in western Massachusetts. It is likely that he saw this quiet place, in spite of its hardships, as offering him the chance to set to paper the great theological tasks he felt needed immediately to be done. No sooner had he settled into this wilderness community with his twelve children and his exhausted wife, than he sat down to write what succeeding generations would think was his finest work: the "enquiry" into the *Freedom of the Will*. This is in some ways a puzzling and forbidding book. There is nothing to indicate that he had been excited into writing it by a recent controversy, or even by the recent publication of one or another book, and yet it is highly polemical and often angry in its mood. Unlike most of his other works, its organization or overall design is haphazard, giving the impression that he took many years to write it. However, according to Sereno Dwight's calculation, it was written in four and one-half months. This moved Dwight to remark that "so far as I am aware, no similar example, of power and rapidity united, is to be found in the annals of Mental effort."[13] Dwight's enthusiasm ought to be tempered with the fact that Edwards' miscellaneous writings, from the time of his "Notes on the Mind," are full of references to the problem of the freedom of the will. Indeed, it should be seen that this is a book he was writing most of his mature life.

How then shall we read it? It is evident that Edwards was deeply alarmed by the rapid growth of Arminianism in America. In one respect the book was designed to destroy this great Calvinist heresy at its roots. But if we take this to be its chief intention then we have every right to regard the whole effort as trivial, if only because it was concerned to show the illegitimacy of positions which would not have survived anyway. But there is something more to the book than mere diatribe; the

[13] *Works of President Edwards,* ed. Sereno E. Dwight (New York: S. Converse, 1829–1830), I, 553.

sound of its guns should not take our attention from the fact that underneath all its surface action there is a doctrine of man in the quiet but steady process of construction. This deeper purpose of the book is stated in Edwards' introduction:

> As religion is the great business, for which we are created, and on which our happiness depends; and as religion consists in an intercourse between ourselves and our Maker; and so has its foundation in God's nature and ours, and in the relation that God and we stand into each other; therefore a true knowledge of both must be needful in order to true religion.[14]

There is a telling similarity between this statement and the sentence with which John Calvin began his great *Institutes:* "Nearly all the wisdom we possess, that is to say, true and sound wisdom, consists of two parts: the knowledge of God and of ourselves."[15] Like Calvin, Edwards saw the necessity of making an intellectual journey that would take him through the very heart of the Christian faith. But the *Freedom of the Will* is not a summa of Christian doctrine; in fact, it does not deal with our knowledge of God at all. Calvin thought it did not matter whether one began with God or with man, but when he decided to begin with God the doctrine of man was swallowed by the doctrine of God. Edwards had learned the necessity of clearing the ground with basic distinctions preliminary to the construction of doctrine proper; he knew that imprecision in the basic presuppositions would bring great confusion into a theological system. Therefore, the *Freedom of the Will,* the book he took a lifetime to write, set forth the fundamental propositions of our knowledge of man. It is on the validity of these propositions that he had been resting the whole of his theological thought.

The knowledge of man, Edwards says in the beginning of

---

[14] *Freedom of the Will* (New Haven, 1957), ed. Paul Ramsey, p. 133.
[15] *Calvin: Institutes of the Christian Religion,* ed. John T. McNeill, trans. Ford Lewis Battles (2 vols.; Philadelphia, 1960), I, i, 1.

this inquiry, "consists chiefly in right apprehensions concerning those two chief faculties of our nature, the *understanding* and *will.*"[16] When he turns to consider these two "faculties" we are freshly reminded of the enduring influence of John Locke on his thought. When Locke surveyed the doctrine of the soul as he had received it out of the Middle Ages he saw, in a moment of great clarity, that far too much attention had been given to the separate faculties.

> For, if it be reasonable to suppose and talk of faculties as distinct beings that can act, (as we do, when we say the will orders, and the will is free,) it is fit that we should make a speaking faculty, and a walking faculty, and a dancing faculty, by which these actions are produced, which are but several modes of motion; as well as we make the will and understanding to be faculties, by which the actions of choosing and perceiving are produced, which are but several modes of thinking.[17]

Locke concluded this line of reasoning with the well-known remark that in the "inquiry about liberty, I think the question is not proper, *whether the will be free,* but *whether the man be free.*"[18]

It is Edwards' consistent use of this teaching which constitutes the heart of his refutation of the Arminian doctrine insofar as it rests on the theory of the self-determination of the will. The notion that the will can determine itself requires that there be two wills in the soul; at the very least, it makes it necessary for us to think of the will so related to itself that it can be its own will.

> If the will be determined, there is a determiner. This must be supposed to be intended even by them that say, the will

16 *Freedom of the Will,* p. 133.

17 *An Essay Concerning Human Understanding,* ed. Alexander Campbell Fraser (New York, 1959), II, xxi, 17.

18 *Ibid.,* II, xxi, 21.

determines itself. If it be so, the will is both determiner and determined; it is a cause that acts and produces effects upon itself, and is the object of its own influence and action.[19]

On this basis, the very argument for the freedom of the will disproves itself, because it shows that the will cannot move unless it is moved by a previous expression of the will, in which case it is not free. If we "should suppose a long chain," Edwards says in his refutation of this view,

> of ten thousand links, so connected that if the first link moves, it will move the next, and that the next, . . . it appears that the motion of no one, nor the direction of its motion, is from any self-moving or self-determining power in the chain, any more than if every link were immediately moved by something that did not belong to the chain. If the will be not free in the first act, which causes the next, then neither is it free in the next, which is caused by that first act: . . . Thus, this Arminian notion of liberty of the will, consisting in the will's self-determination, is repugnant to itself, and shuts itself wholly out of the world.[20]

Edwards sensed that the Arminian doctrine, like Locke's account of the process of thinking, appealed for credulity on the basis of an implicit metaphor: the chain of countless links. The Arminians intended to controvert what they thought was the Calvinist view that each act of the will had its efficient cause immediately preceding it in time, like links of the chain running indefinitely back into the past and therefore indefinitely on into the future, but they could not escape the metaphor in the defense of their own position. To say that the will is its own will is only playing with words; it is not genuinely to overturn the ancient habit of conceiving the soul as a mechanical device requiring an external agent.

Edwards' criticism of the Arminian position may seem too

[19] *Freedom of the Will*, p. 141.   [20] *Ibid.*, p. 174.

easy; it may appear to be a victory with meagre spoils, but if we take full stock of the fact that Jacob Arminius and his followers were *Calvinist* heretics, we might be able to see that Edwards has put himself in command of a much more comprehensive field. The rejection of Arminianism came from the denial that the will had a will. But this confusion of wills does not begin with a Calvinist heretic; it is present in Calvin himself. In his discussion of the operations of God on the soul Calvin decided characteristically to sweep away all sophistry and declare boldly that scripture means what it says: God hardened Pharaoh's heart. But that is not all. When God finished this he "delivered his heart to Satan to be confirmed in obstinacy."[21] Similarly did Luther and Augustine see the matter. Both used the simile of the will as a horse with either God or Satan as its rider. It is, of course, true that for all of these theologians the sinful man *also acts according to his own will.* Man is always said to sin voluntarily, by his own desire, simultaneously to his being determined to it by God. But no theologian by Edwards' day had succeeded in stating this relationship of wills in a way that did not lead either to nonsense or contradiction. The Arminians opted for nonsense by having man be his own rider; thereby making it necessary for that rider to have a rider to have a rider, etc. The orthodox Protestants left it with a contradiction: man is both rider and horse —and so is God.

By putting himself under the Lockean teaching that the proper question is not whether the *will* be free, but whether the *man* be free, Edwards was in a position to formulate the nature of man's relationship to God that followed neither the Arminians nor the traditional Calvinists. By way of a preliminary definition, Edwards writes that the will "is plainly, that by which the mind chooses anything. The faculty of the will is that faculty or power or principle of mind by which

21 *Institutes of the Christian Religion,* I, ii, 4.

it is capable of choosing: an act of the will is the same as an act of choosing or choice."[22] This is the conventional definition; and it is not until we ask why the will chooses, and what determines which object it will choose, that we find Edwards moving out into his own territory. He answers that "it is that motive, which, as it stands in the view of the mind, is the strongest, that determines the will."[23] A motive is not something operating on the will from the outside, like one link on another or a rider on a horse, but it is rather the *view* of something external to the will.

Edwards has eliminated the mechanistic description of the will's operations, and replaced it with the living human mind. The human mind is not an inert piece of equipment that will wait in idleness until it is activated by an external agent; it is life itself. It is the source of our humanness; it is not a thing at all, but an action; it is our viewing of the world, and our judging it; it is the richly interpenetrated confluence of our passions and fears, our prejudice and our habits. To say that the mind is any one thing, or that it operates according to any one procedure, is obviously impossible. To look directly into the human mind is to look directly into a mystery which cannot be exhausted by any amount of metaphorical descriptions. That the mind is located in the brain, or that it is identical to some physical process, is manifest nonsense. Should we cut open the skull and analyze by the subtlest scientific methods the structure and composition of that organ we should know no more about the ideas and thoughts and values that man had, than if we had attempted, by studying the leg of a cadaver, to determine where he had wandered over the face of this earth. It is this mystery which stands directly in Edwards' view. He knows that when he comes to that final statement of the nature of the human will he must so state it that it will comprehend the whole situation of man as an ever alive par-

---

[22] *Freedom of the Will*, p. 137.   [23] *Ibid.*, p. 141.

ticipant in the rushing currents of history. He makes the statement with disarming coolness: "The will always is as the greatest apparent good is."[24]

There are several arresting consequences to this statement. The first is that it effectively eliminates from our talking about the will the necessity of referring to determinacy. As Edwards explains,

> I have rather chosen to express myself thus, that the will always *is* as the greatest apparent good, or as what appears most agreeable, is, than to say that the will is *determined* by the greatest apparent good, or by what seems most agreeable; because an appearing most agreeable or pleasing to the mind, and the mind's preferring and choosing, seem hardly to be properly and perfectly distinct.[25]

Another consequence is that it puts man out into the thrust and rush of the historical process without giving him any access to eternal verities or realities that can permanently withstand the change of the moment. Man is restricted to that which *appears* to him; he cannot go behind the appearance to the *real* thing. Here we can see how the boy still lives in the man; for there is in this statement the same intellectual clarity that caused young Edwards to reject Locke's "magic onions." We must emphasize again that when Edwards uses the term "apparent" he does not mean to set it in contrast with something "real" and non-apparent; he means rather to draw our attention to the fact that it is our *view* of the thing, and not the thing itself, that counts in the action of our will. In this sense the term "apparent" is equivalent to the term "visible." That which falls outside our view, therefore, has no effect on our mind.[26]

If Edwards arrives at this place in his thought out of the original impulse of avoiding the contradictory and nonsensical consequences of the talk about determinacy, should we not

[24] *Ibid.*, p. 142.   [25] *Ibid.*, p. 144.   [26] Cf. *ibid.*, p. 142.

now say that he has put himself into a determinism far more suffocating than the traditional Calvinist formulation of it? Has he not now bound man by a billion diaphanous causes to the fortuitous and superficial events of a reality that extends no farther than the limits of his own understanding? In anticipation of this question, or one like it, Edwards proposes a distinction between different kinds of causes. By "cause," he writes, he means "any antecedent with which a consequent event is so connected, that it truly belongs to the reason why the proposition which affirms that event, is true."[27] The distinction between kinds of causes comes from his recognition that there are propositions about different kinds of events, and therefore different kinds of reasons for those propositions being true or false. There are propositions about *events in the world,* and propositions about *events in the mind.* The former deal with what Edwards, following terminology Locke had proposed,[28] calls "natural causes" and the latter "moral causes." When men are under natural causes "they feel pain when their bodies are wounded; they see objects presented before them in a clear light, when their eyes are opened."[29] By moral causes he means "the strength of inclination, or motives, and the connection which there is in many cases between these, and such certain volitions and actions."[30] Moral causes apply uniquely to human nature. Indeed, it might even be said that moral causation is identical with man's humanness; it is of the essence of man that he has a capacity for "being influenced in his actions by moral inducements or motives, exhibited to the view of the understanding and reason."[31]

> And herein does very much consist that image of God wherein he made man (which we read of in Gen. 1: 26, 27 and ch. 9:6), by which God distinguished man from

[27] *Ibid.,* p. 181.
[28] *An Essay Concerning Human Understanding* (see note 17), IV, v, 11.
[29] *Freedom of the Will,* p. 157.
[30] *Ibid.,* p. 156.   [31] *Ibid.,* p. 165.

the beasts, viz., in those faculties and principles of nature, whereby he is capable of moral agency.[32]

Here is the distinction which the Arminians and the Calvinists never successfully worked into their description of the will's operations. They insisted on using the model of *natural* causation to account for what was essentially *moral* causation.

It is essential to our explication of Edwards' position on this matter that we be able to state in ordinary language what he means by "moral" causation. It would certainly preserve the mystery of the human soul, and it would satisfy Edwards' desire that we "speak in the old way as truly and properly as ever," if we summarized his teaching with this proposition: *To say that all mental events are determined is merely to say that whatever a man does, he does for a reason.* In reference to mental events, the *cause* of a man's action is the same as his *reason* for that action.

We can see here, too, how Edwards continues to live in the world of unboxed beetles. When he reads natural causation out of moral behavior he eliminates from the mind the unseen causes that operate there. When, in our interpretation of his position, we say that persons always have reasons for doing what they do, it is presupposed that there can be such reasons only in given contextual circumstances. The reason a man steals is that he covets the possessions of another which he can acquire in no other way. But such a reason is possible only where there is private or restricted property. We can usually look at a man's context and ascertain the reasons for his actions. Sometimes it might take extended investigation or unusually sensitive understanding, but, at least according to Edwards' notion of the soul's operations, it can always be done. Morality for Edwards is totally visible.

If the Arminian doctrine of self-determinacy shuts itself out

---

[32] *Ibid.*, p. 166.

of the world on the *philosophical* grounds that it is either self-contradictory or nonsensical, there are also *ethical* and *religious* reasons why it is untenable. Self-determinacy is thought to be a kind of freedom on the basis that there is an event *within* the mind not controlled by anything *outside* the mind. On their side, the Arminians felt they had strong ethical reasons for the truth of their position inasmuch as it seems necessary that there be freedom in order that there might be culpability; a person cannot be held guilty for that in which he had no choice. One of the defenders of this doctrine, a Dr. Whitby,[33] happened to be in Edwards' path when this point came to discussion. Such freedom as Whitby wanted, Edwards saw, would not sustain praise and blame, but would cancel it out. "For if an impossibility of avoiding sin wholly excuses a man; then, for the same reason, its being difficult to avoid it excuses him in part; and this just in proportion to the degree of difficulty."[34] This gives Edwards just the right formula, since he can now say that for Whitby the more one is inclined to sin, the more he is excused from it. Sin is its own excuse from sin.[35]

This understanding of freedom introduces into the moral structure an action of the human mind separate from the acts of the whole man and asks that the man be judged on the basis of the invisible events inside his soul; and the apologist for freedom is, in Edwards' judgment, the more passionate when that freedom is the more invisible—that is, when sin is the greatest, the claims of freedom are thought the most valid. Freedom of the will is therefore more than a philosophical error; it also provides the basis for ethical irresponsibility, for the privilege of being bracketed out of the corruptibility and finitude of historical existence. Man is therefore allowed to

[33] By the time of Edwards' writing Daniel Whitby had written the most vigorous defense of the Arminian position in his *A Discourse* (London: A. Ward & R. Hett, 1735).

[34] *Freedom of the Will*, p. 297.   [35] *Ibid.*, p. 297ff.

disengage himself from the human context, and to say that the reasons for his actions are not the visible historical ones. It is Edwards' design to put man squarely back into the dimensions of history.

If the Arminian doctrine is philosophically absurd and ethically irresponsible, it is also *religiously* feckless and even blasphemous. Once a person has supposed that he can put himself into the alcove of his soul without any real connection with what passes by on the outside, he takes his relationship with God out of history. Now there is no public act of God—no commandment, no moral government, no ecclesiastical institution—that can in the least influence our relationship to him if we do not want it to. Our business with God will be *where we like it* and *when we choose*. It will be remembered that this is precisely the position Solomon Stoddard took in the debate over qualifications for communion.[36] With memorable eloquence Stoddard's grandson now writes that according to this conception God is

> a being, who, instead of being absolutely immutable, must necessarily be the subject of infinitely the most numerous acts of repentance, and changes of intention, of any being whatsoever; for this plain reason, that his vastly extensive charge comprehends an infinitely greater number of those things which are to him contingent and uncertain. In such a situation, he must have little else to do, but to mend broken links as well as he can, and be rectifying his disjointed frame and disordered movements, in the best manner the case will allow. The supreme Lord of all things must needs be under great and miserable disadvantages, in governing the world which he has made, and has the care of, through his being utterly unable to find out things of chief importance, which hereafter shall befall his system; which if he did but know, he might make seasonable provision for. . . . And it is in the power of man, on these

[36] See above, pp. 24ff.

principles, by his devices, purposes and actions, thus to dis-
appoint God, break his measures, make him continually to
change his mind, subject him to vexation, and bring him
into confusion.[37]

There are two concluding and summarizing remarks that
must be salvaged from this discussion of Edwards' doctrine
of man. The first has to do with man himself. Edwards puts
understanding and will at the center of man, refusing to analyze them as though they were pieces of mechanical equipment. He will insist that the understanding and the will are
not separate faculties, but interdependent functions of a unified
soul. Therefore, since the will can have no cause but the understanding, it can be said that, in some sense, the will is determined. But in order to circumvent the erroneous tendency
to conceive of this determination in mechanical terms, we have
paraphrased Edwards' position in the expression that *everything a man does he does for a reason.* At the same time, Edwards is teaching us that man's mind, or his understanding,
cannot extend beyond the strictly historical limits of his experience. It is not his intuition of trans-historical verities, but
his experiential perception of the greatest good as it appears
to him in the context of the world, that determines what he
does as a man. Even his reasons are historical.

The second concluding remark has to do with the surprising
restriction this lays on man's relationship with God. Since it
it not merely a matter of physical necessity that man is held to
the relativities of historical existence, but either contradictory
or nonsensical to suppose anything else, it is unthinkable that
God would relate himself to man in any other way than
through man's experience of the world. It is inconsistent with
Edwards' doctrine of man to suppose that man could relate
himself to God through a private mystical communication, or

[37] *Freedom of the Will,* pp. 253f.

even through the universal validities of reason. It is also inconsistent to think that God could be understood by a person without that understanding having in turn a direct impact on the person's life. We cannot talk about man and God apart from what man *actually does* in the world. But along with the mechanistic view of the soul's operation we must abandon any such causal terms to discuss the manner of God's influence on man. According to the old doctrines of predestination it was necessary to say that God *caused* the will of man to go in one direction or another; but in the *Freedom of the Will* Edwards has given shape to an altogether new way of talking about the will of God: God can have no part in determining what man actually does in the world unless he becomes man's reason for doing it.

IV.

A BLAZING SUN
FOR THE BLACK
EMPTINESS OF DEATH

The *Freedom of the Will* laid the basic propositions about the nature of man, but it by no means told all that Edwards had to say about man. Once it has been explained *how* man wills, it is necessary clearly to perceive *what* he wills. There is no one even slightly familiar with Edwards' thought who does not know that when it comes to the question as to what man actually wills, he exercises a passionate and consistent opinion. "Children's coming into the world naked and filthy in their blood," Edwards once recorded in his private notes, "is to signify the spiritual nakedness and pollution of nature and wretchedness of condition with which they are born."[1] Attached inseparably to his teaching on the nature of the will is the doctrine of original sin.

"The Great Christian Doctrine of Original Sin," as Edwards referred to it in the title of his last book, has always been a prominent piece in the inherited baggage of the Calvinist tradition, but it would be a serious misinterpretation of

[1] Perry Miller, ed., *Images or Shadows of Divine Things* (New Haven, 1948), No. 10, p. 45.

the function of this doctrine in Edwards' thought if we assume he believed it simply *because* Calvin taught it, or even that he believed it *as* Calvin taught it. He did not give the great Christian doctrine his assent until he had reasons in the experience of his life to think it was true.

It is worth noting that while young Jonathan was hearing the doctrine regularly expounded by his father, and by his teachers at Yale, it almost never appears in his childhood writings. His attention fell more eagerly on the sublime nature of God than on the corruption man was making of his life. Before he had been entered into Yale College he had already worked out a sort of ontological proof for the existence of God which is significant not for its logical force, but for the way it reflects the confident youthful enthusiasm of propositions freshly seized upon.

> That there should be absolutely nothing at all is utterly impossible, the Mind Can Let it stretch its Conceptions ever so much to bring it self to Conceive of a state of Perfect nothing. . . . So that we see it is necessary some being should Eternally be and tis a more palpable Contradiction still to say that there must be being somewhere and not otherwhere for the words absolute nothing, and where, Contradict each other; and besides it Gives a great shock to the mind to think of pure nothing being in any one place, as it Does to think of it in all and it is self evident that there Can be nothing in one place as well as in another and so if there Can be in one there Can be in all. So that we see this necessary eternal being must be infinite and Omnipresent.[2]

With the enviable innocence of one still unacquainted with the crookedness of both the world and his own heart, Edwards was looking straight into the blazing sun. The rapture of these

---

[2] "Of Being," Clarence H. Faust and Thomas H. Johnson, eds. *Jonathan Edwards* (New York, 1962), p. 18.

early moments is expressed nowhere better than in the nostal-
gic account of his conversion written down by himself some
twenty years afterward. In his experience of being suddenly
"wrapt and swallowed up in God,"[3] he imagined his soul to be

> like such a little white flower as we see in the spring of the
> year; low and humble on the ground, opening its bosom
> to receive the pleasant beams of the sun's glory; rejoicing as
> it were in a calm rapture; diffusing around a sweet fra-
> grancy; standing peacefully and lovingly, in the midst of
> other flowers round about; all in like manner opening their
> bosoms, to drink in the light of the sun.[4]

So long as the brilliance of God illumined his world, he could
behold there nothing but beauty; and in the beauty and order
of the world he could see nothing but the immediate presence
of God.

> The being of God may be argued from the desirableness
> and the need of it. Thus we see in all nature every where that
> great necessities are supplied . . . The young of insects they
> are not able to provide for themselves nor do their dams
> take care of them, but they by instinct are laid where they
> have their food round about them. Camels are forced being
> in dry countrys to go long without water and they have a
> large vessel within them which being filled supplies them a
> long time. And so it is in every thing.[5]

In a later entry in the *Miscellanies* he says that to suppose all
of this beauty and order came about by chance is as silly as
supposing that

> in the showers of rain that fall out of the clouds on all the
> face of the earth for a whole year the drops should uni-

---

[3] "Personal Narrative," *ibid.,* p. 60.   [4] *Ibid.,* p. 63.
[5] *Miscellanies,* Yale MSS., No. 274. It should be remarked that several small
changes in punctuation have slightly altered the rendering of the passages
quoted here from the Yale manuscripts of the *Miscellanies.* On the whole, however, our reading follows Professor Thomas A. Schafer's typescript of the original mss.

versally fall in order on the ground so as to describe such
figures that would be Roman letters in such exact order
as to be Vergi[l's] Eneid written on every acre of ground
all over the world or so as exactly to write the history
of the world and all nations & families in it through all
ages without departing from truth in one fact or minutest
circumstance.[6]

No chronicle of Edwards' intellectual development can
overlook the amazing fact that he was the only manchild born
to a family of eleven children. We should be allowed to guess
that not only was he the subject of rather special attention
particularly on the part of his father, but that there presided
in his home, by reason of its Calvinist strictness and overwhelming femininity, an uncommon combination of order and
tenderness. All the pieces of young Edwards' universe were
precisely located and reasonably connected, and obviously de-
lightful to live in. Therefore, when he attempted to describe
his experience of this world in philosophical terms he reached
all the more earnestly for such concepts as rectitude, order,
harmony, beauty, and excellency. One of the more important
entries in the "Notes on the Mind" was entitled *Excellency*.

There has nothing been more without a definition, than
Excellency; although it be what we are more concerned
with, than any thing else whatsoever; yea, we are concerned
with nothing else. But what is this Excellency? Wherein is
one thing excellent, and another evil; one beautiful, and
another deformed? Some have said that all Excellency is
Harmony, Symmetry, or *Proportion;* But they have not yet
explained it. We would know, Why Proportion is more
excellent than Disproportion; that is, why Proportion is
pleasant to the mind, and Disproportion unpleasant? Proportion is a thing that may be explained yet further. It is an
Equality, or *Likeness of Ratios;* so that it is the Equality,

that makes the Proportion. Excellency therefore seems to consist in *Equality*. Thus, if there be two perfect *equal* circles or globes, together, there is something more of beauty than if they were of *unequal,* disproportionate magnitudes. And if two *parallel* lines be drawn, the beauty is greater, than if they were *obliquely* inclined without proportion, because there is equality of distance.[7]

But the summer of Edwards' childhood came inevitably to its end. The more he saw of life the more he could see that a crippling frost had fallen on the garden God had fashioned in the full light of his glory. No longer could he see men turning upward "to drink in the light of the sun." Their lives were not upright, but bent, looking not upon the heavens, but upon themselves and the dull earth in which they are momentarily rooted. "I have now, abundant reason to be convinced," he wrote dejectedly into the diary he kept at Yale, "of the troublesomeness and vexation of the world, and that it never will be another kind of world."[8] By now he had fastened himself to the hard view of man that would persist to the end of his life. "Many kinds of brute animals are esteemed very noxious and destructive," he said in *The Great Christian Doctrine of Original Sin Defended,*

many of them very fierce, voracious, and many very poisonous, and the destroying of them has always been looked upon as a public benefit; but have not mankind been a thousand times as hurtful and destructive as any one of them, yea, as all the noxious beasts, birds, fishes, and reptiles in the earth, air, and water, put together, at least of all kinds of animals that are visible.[9]

So far as the definition of sin is concerned, there is no departure from the traditional understanding in Edwards'

7 Faust and Johnson, *Jonathan Edwards,* pp. 30f.
8 "Diary," Faust and Johnson, p. 51.
9 *Works* (see Chap. One, note 7), II, 347f.

thought. Sin is a state of enmity between man and God, and between man and man. "All sin may be resolved into hatred of God and our neighbor. . . . Sin is of such a nature, that it wishes ill, and aims at ill to God and man; but to God especially. It strikes at God; it would, if it could, procure his misery and death."[10] In an interesting entry in the *Miscellanies* he explains that "the sin of crucifying X seems to have been designed of God to be a representative sin of mankind in general," for in this act it "appeared that sin aimed at nothing short of the life of God that in its nature it was a murderer of G."[11]

It is significant that while Edwards became disillusioned with the nature of the world and the unevenness of man's existence in it, he did not abandon the sublime sense of order and beauty that had captured him as a youth. Therefore, sin must first be understood as it pertains to the rectitude by which all things have been constituted.

> Now the rectitude of human nature and of rational beings most certainly is that they should be most highly affected with the highest excellencies, and less affected with lower excellencies. . . . But we know, as well as we know that we have being, that this rectitude is not the present state of human nature but the right contrary, in all universally. . . .[12]

It was unthinkable to Edwards that God's orderly relationship with the world be disturbed; thus, though it would seem that sin would be a violent disruption of it, even this must in the end be understood as having its place in the overall excellency with which God governs. The importance of this point in our interpretation of Edwards cannot be exaggerated. It is by a logical extension of his youthful understanding of God that he comes in mature life to such a terrifying conception of

---

[10] *Works,* I, 584.   [11] *Miscellanies,* Yale MSS., No. 762.
[12] *Miscellanies,* Yale MSS., No. 34.

man's stance before his maker. In light of the fact that God governs the natural world according to the "most perfect exactness or proportion harmony equity & beauty," Edwards felt it was self-evident that God "will maintain the most strict & perfect justice in proportion & fitness in what he does as the Governour of the moral world."[13] Indeed, this is

> what the consciences of all men do naturally declare. There is nothing that men know sooner, after they come to the exercise of their reason, than that, when they have done wickedness, they deserve punishment.[14]

When the order of the garden is disturbed by the flowers within it, it is necessary that the gardener restore it; and how may he restore it except by undoing that which was done and according to the same measure?

But what is the measure of sin? With his own eye on that great God in whom he longed to be swallowed up as a child, Edwards says with a logical force that belies the passion in which that logic originates, "if God be infinitely excellent in himself, then he is infinitely worthy to be loved."[15] The conclusion to this line of argument is obvious, and he took it to that conclusion not once, but many times in his preaching. In his "habitual and great solemnity, looking and speaking as in the presence of God,"[16] he exclaimed that

> a crime is more or less heinous, according as we are under greater or less obligations to the contrary. . . . So that sin against God, being a violation of infinite obligations, must be a crime infinitely heinous, and so deserving of infinite punishment.[17]

Edwards is unafraid of the charge that to destroy that which he created God is forced to cancel out the validity of his own

---

13 *Miscellanies,* Yale MSS., No. 1196.   14 *Works,* I, 584.

15 *Works,* II, 332.

16 Thomas Prince, quoted in Ola Winslow, *Jonathan Edwards 1703–1758* (New York, 1961), p. 129.

17 *Works,* IV, 228.

work. In a sermon he called "Wicked Men Useful in Their Destruction Only," he said that those who bring forth no fruit may be useful to God as a fruitless tree is to the gardener who will cut it down for firewood. Wicked men "are fit for nothing else," but they *are* fit for that.[18]

Thus far we have examined Edwards' understanding of the nature of sin as it is viewed over against the infinite beauty of the divine being, and the excellency with which he has ordered all things. Now we must examine it more explicitly for the part man has in it.

It will directly contribute to the clarity of our view of Edwards here if we take account of the dimensions of this problem as they are manifest in Calvin. On the one hand, Calvin wanted to define original sin as a "corruption of our nature,"[19] in order that our culpability might not be easily dodged; and yet, on the other hand, he did not want to teach that sin was so innate to our nature that it should not be we, but our Creator, who is finally to blame, since it is he who made us as we are. Furthermore, if sin is to be understood as merely a natural corruption then Calvin would have been defenseless against the Roman doctrine that righteousness is a *superadditum* to a presently imperfect nature; and this, in the Reformer's judgment, would cast even greater odium on God, since it would imply that his original work could be improved. Therefore, Calvin decides he must hammer through this problem by a direct verbal blow whether or not it destroys the logic of the situation at the same time.

> . . . man is corrupted through natural vitiation, but a vitiation that did not flow from nature. We deny that it has flowed from nature in order to indicate that it is an adventitious quality which comes upon man rather than a substan-

---

[18] *Works*, IV, 304.
[19] *Institutes of the Christian Religion*, ed. John T. McNeill, trans. Ford Lewis Battles (Philadelphia, 1960), II, i, 8.

tial property which has been implanted from the beginning. Yet we call it natural in order that no man may think that anyone obtains it through bad conduct, since it holds all men fast by hereditary right.[20]

It is clearly inadequate to resolve this dilemma by saying that man's corruption is both natural and not natural. The Calvinist tradition therefore inherited from its *Urvater* the annoying question as to the precise connection between human sinfulness and human nature.

It was exactly this question Edwards decided he must take up. In his defense of the great Christian doctrine of original sin, the last book he was personally to see through the press, he states at the outset that

As all moral qualities, all principles of virtue or vice, lie in the disposition of the heart, I shall consider whether we have any evidence, that the heart of man is naturally of a corrupt and evil disposition.[21]

We should not be surprised that he is able to find an abundance of evidence, both in the experience of man and in the testimony of scripture. This pushes us back then to the question as to how that evil disposition got into the heart. Edwards is insistent that Adam, until he ate the forbidden fruit, had "been perfectly righteous, righteous from the first moment of his existence, and consequently, created, or brought into existence righteous."[22] At the same time, he is careful not to say that Adam was *free* to be either righteous or sinful, as though each of these options was equally available, for this would have plunged him into the confusion of the Arminian position. In Edwards' view of the matter

Adam was brought into existence capable of acting immediately, as a moral agent, and therefore he was immediately

[20] *Institutes of the Christian Religion*, I, i, 11.
[21] *Works*, II, 309.   [22] *Works*, II, 385.

> under a rule of *right* action: he was obliged to act right
> as soon as he existed, he was obliged even then to be *in-
> clined* to act right[23]

But still he does not succeed in keeping confusion out of his
own position as he attempts to explain how Adam passed
from righteousness to sin. Elsewhere he is bold enough to argue
that since we know that the sin of crucifying Christ was foreordained of God in his decree, and since this is "the head sin,
and representative of the sin of men in general," it is therefore a "clear argument, that all the sins of men are foreordained
and ordered by a wise providence."[24] But he is simply unable
to give such direct agency to God in the case of Adam's first
sin. Instead, he opts for an ancient method of dodging the
discomfort of this moment: the distinction between God's per-
mitting will and his ordaining will. Ignoring Calvin's disdain-
ful charge that this distinction is the merest sophistry,[25]
Edwards explains that

> the first arising or existing of that evil disposition in the
> heart of Adam, was by God's *permission;* who could have
> prevented it, if he had pleased, by *giving* such influences of
> his Spirit, as would have been absolutely effectual to hinder
> it; which, it is plain in fact, he did withold: and whatever
> mystery may be supposed in the affair, yet no Christian will
> presume to say, it was not in perfect consistence with God's
> *holiness* and *righteousness,* notwithstanding Adam had been
> guilty of no offense before.[26]

Once he has Adam awash in his sins, a certain clarity re-
turns to the discussion. Looking back on the originally righteous Adam, it can be said that "when God made man at first,
he implanted in him two kinds of principles." The first Edwards refers to as the *natural* principles; these are "the prin-

---

[23] *Ibid.*   [24] *Works,* II, 517.
[25] *Institutes of the Christian Religion,* I, xviii, 1.
[26] *Works,* II, 483.

ciples of mere human nature; such as self-love, with those natural appetites and passions, which belong to the *nature of man,* in which his love to his own liberty, honor and pleasure, were exercised. . . ." The natural principles man always has with him; they cannot be removed without removing his very humanity. The second kind of principles Edwards calls *supernatural.* As God implanted them in Adam they "were spiritual, holy, and divine, summarily comprehended in divine love; wherein consisted the spiritual image of God, and man's righteousness and true holiness; which are called in Scripture the *divine nature.*" The supernatural principles depend entirely "on man's union and communion with God, or divine communications and influences of God's Spirit: which, though withdrawn, and man's nature forsaken of these principles, human nature would be human nature still. . ." On this basis, Edwards can say that man's corruption is natural without impugning the original work of God, for there is nothing faulty in the natural principles themselves. It is only that they were intended "to be wholly subordinate and subservient" to the supernatural principles. "And while things continued thus, all things were in excellent order, peace, and beautiful harmony, and in the proper and perfect state."[27] It will remain for us to determine in another place whether the supernatural principles can be added through regeneration without disturbing the basic structure of human nature. For the moment, we can at least say that Edwards has succeeded in asserting that sin is a natural corruption.

There is still something to be learned about the character of the natural principles, however, for the term "self-love" which is used to describe them is much too ambiguous. In fact, it suggests the very sort of double agency of the will that Edwards attacked in the Arminians: in order to love itself, the self must have a self, etc. This problem is not dealt with

[27] *Works,* II, 476f.

in the volume on original sin, but in another briefer and subtler book which he was writing in the same period, he supplies a definition of self-love which provides a clear transition from the doctrine of the will to the doctrine of original sin. We recall that his fundamental thesis with regard to human agency was that "the will is as the most apparent good is." The will is not pushed by another will, but it follows that which the understanding has seized upon as the most desirable, or the most beautiful. In the *Dissertation on the Nature of True Virtue* he says that self-love, just like true virtue, is drawn by the beauty of its object; the difference is that what is beauty for self-love is not beauty for true virtue.

> There is a general and particular beauty. By a particular beauty, I mean that by which a thing appears beautiful when considered only with regard to its connection with, and tendency to, some particular things within a limited, and as it were a private sphere. And a general beauty is that by which a thing appears beautiful when viewed most perfectly, comprehensively and universally, with regard to all its tendencies, and its connections with every thing to which it stands related. The former may be without and against the latter.[28]

In our investigation of Edwards' teaching on the nature of the will we found that he had put us into the midst of a thorough relativism, that he had restricted man to the limited sphere of his own understanding and had left him no access to universally valid truths. We can now see that he wants to identify these natural limitations of man with his sinfulness. Edwards is saying, in essence, that it is only the *natural* inclination of a man that he look for the greatest good somewhere within the private sphere of his own life. It was only natural for the church in Northampton to act on the basis of what it could understand and value within its own community,

28 *The Nature of True Virtue,* ed. William K. Frankena (Ann Arbor, Michigan, 1960), pp. 2f.

ignoring its comprehensive and universal connections with the historic church of all Christendom or with American society as a whole. It is only natural that Americans, like the citizens of any other nation, have taken their form of government and style of living to be, of all peoples, the most desirable. It is only natural that a man see great beauty in the institutions of a society which has guaranteed a superior status for whatever race or class he chanced to have been born into. It is only natural that, surrounded by sophisticated comforts and persons as pleasant in intercourse as they are agreeable in taste, a man should strongly prefer retaining what he possesses to satisfying the angry, desperate cries of need on the part of those who must live in the squalor of poverty and ignorance. It is only natural, it is only human, that a man love those things most that serve him best. Therefore, from Edwards' point of view, to be human is to be sinful; to be human is to be in a state of enmity against God and man.

It is interesting to note that this rather extreme but consistent view has relieved Edwards of one of the difficult theological problems facing every fashioner of Christian doctrine. It has always been clear that sinfulness is in some sense *inherited,* but the defenders of original sin have always had to answer to the reasonable charge that God was therefore punishing Adam's progeny for no sin of their own, but only for being born. Now if sinfulness is to be equated with humanness then so long as one human being will spring from the loins of another, there will be a tendency to sin. Edwards can in this way avoid attributing to God sheer arbitrariness, since if men are polluted by their very nature through the normal process of birth, "the sin of apostasy is not theirs, merely because God *imputes* it to them; but it is *truly* and *properly* theirs, and on that *ground,* God imputes it to them."[29] If it were the case

29 *Works,* II, 493.

that the sin of Adam, either in its pollution or punishment, reached none but himself, any more than the sin of any other man, it would be no more proper to say, that *by one man sin entered into the world*, than if it should be inquired, how mankind came into America, and there had anciently been a ship of the Phenicians wrecked at sea, and a single man of the crew was driven ashore on this continent, and here died as soon as he reached the shore, it should be said, *by that one mankind came into America*.[30]

Another way to articulate Edwards' view in this matter is to say that man's sinfulness is identical to his historicality. There is nothing outside history that caused him to sin—neither a free, self-determining act of his will, nor the imputative judgment of God acting independently of man's particular situation. But, on the same account, there is nothing within history that can get man out of his sinfulness. The Arminians, Edwards thought, erred on both sides. Having said that man was not *caused* to do evil by his visible, historical circumstances, but only by his free and uncaused will, they can then argue that the presence of evil in the world was designed by God to embolden the more virtuous inclinations of the free agent.

Edwards' book on original sin was intended chiefly as a defense against a popular work by an American contemporary, John Taylor,[31] who had argued that affliction and death, far from being the consequence of sin only, are "a great benefit, as they increase the vanity of all earthly things, and tend to excite sober reflections, and to induce us to be moderate in gratifying the appetites of the body, and to mortify pride and ambition."[32] Taylor was encouraged to take this position by

---

[30] *Works*, II, 436.

[31] Cf. Clyde Holbrook's account of the controversy surrounding Taylor and his book. "Original Sin and the Enlightenment," *The Heritage of Christian Thought*, ed. Robert E. Cushman and Egil Grislis (New York, 1965), pp. 142ff.

[32] *Works*, II, 374.

the disgust with which he, and most other men, regarded Edwards' unalloyed denigration of human nature. But Edwards could turn their argument back on them, for if this is the reason why God put the stamp of mortality on our lives and delivered us into what "is spoken of in Scripture as the chief of calamities, the most extreme and terrible of all those natural evils, which come on mankind in this world,"[33] then

> is it not strange that it should fall so heavy on infants, who are not capable of making any such improvement of it; so that many more of mankind suffer death in infancy, than in any other equal part of the age of man? Our author sometimes hints, that the death of infants may be for the good of parents, and those that are adult, and may be for the correction and punishment of the sins of parents: but hath God any need of such methods to add to parents' afflictions?[34]

It is at this point that we can see how easily Edwards' doctrine of original sin can be misunderstood. When we hear him insist, as he so frequently does, that "*every* man is *born* into the world in a state of *moral pollution*,"[35] it is a mistake to cast him in the role of a bitter misanthrope cruelly inveighing against even helpless babies for their wretchedness. We should rather hear him crying out, in the names of all men, against the savage limitations and vicissitudes of human existence. Infant mortality is not a proof of the odiousness of infants, but a poignant reminder that it is man's portion, *as man,* to die. This is the permanent and irrevocable character of our existence on this globe, and Edwards is determined not to let us think it is anything else. Death is plainly terrifying, and it is more than wrong-headed, it is cynical and insensitive, to presume that it can serve as a model or a prod to the living.

We have attempted to understand Edwards on the doctrine

[33] *Works*, II, 373.   [34] *Works*, II, 375.
[35] *Works*, II, 472.

of sin first as it appears over against his youthful notions of God's orderly relationship to the world, and secondly as it appears in the context of his adult conclusions on the manner of the soul's operations. In the latter we found that sinfulness was simply identical to humanness. In the former, we found that, according to the rectitude by which God governs all things, there will be an equivalent recompense for the destructiveness that originates in man's enmity toward both God and himself. Edwards will not let us remove either God or man from the historical process, but at the same time he will not let us make God synonymous with the historical process. Because the universe is knit in perfect order, there will be *consequences* to all our actions in it. In this sense, man is not only fully historical, he is also an ethical being. There are strictures set before his actions, and there is the inevitability of praise and blame following them. It is just as true for us as it was for Adam that evil is "not only a *natural* consequence, according to the course of things established by God and the Author of Nature; but it was also a *penal* consequence, or a punishment of his sin."[36] What befalls us in this life comes not by *accident,* but by *desert.* Our relation to evil is not properly to be described in terms of passive victimization, but rather in terms of the intending will; not in terms of what *happens to us,* but in terms of what *we actually do.*

If Edwards did not develop this doctrine out of illicit thirst for the misfortune of others, what then did he intend by it? We observed above that his thought is so structured that it is impossible to leave his doctrine of man without passing through the doctrine of original sin; but where do we go from here? At the beginning of his "*general Defense* of that great important Doctrine," Edwards answers this question himself:

36 *Works,* II, 480.

the great *Salvation* by Christ stands in direct Relation to this *Ruin,* as the remedy to the disease; and the whole *Gospel,* or Doctrine of Salvation, must suppose it; and all real belief, or true notion of that Gospel, must be built upon it.[37]

If Edwards bore nothing in common with the Arminian John Taylor who carelessly suggested that God used suffering and death as a moral example for the living, neither is he to be compared to a Marcus Aurelius who felt he had reached the outer limits of his reflections with his severe view of man's finitude, thus concluding that all the actions of life must be grounded on this ultimate fact. As a child Edwards' soul could gaze only on the brilliant effulgence of God; but as a man he was brought round to look straight into the black emptiness of death. The peculiar power of Edwards' understanding of man's sinfulness lies in the fact that, as a Christian, he believed that the true light has entered into the infinite night of death and has overcome it.

[37] *Works,* II, 307.

V.

A NON-MYTHOLOGICAL
INTERLUDE

*W*e are now at that place in our portrait of Edwards where we must decide how to interpret the one feature of his thought that seems most difficult to reconcile with the modern American intellectual climate: his unquestioned belief in God. He was not simply another philosopher, nor was he just a critic of human society, a gainsayer of man's modest efforts in the struggle to make his sojourn on this earth as pleasant as it is brief. Jonathan Edwards was a Christian theologian who rested the final validity of his thought not on what all men can know by reason, or by the extraordinary labors of wisdom, but on a special kind of knowledge that some men have and others cannot understand. Every interpreter of Edwards is tempted to distinguish between two kinds of material in his thought: the first concerns those subjects which all thinkers may deal with, such as the nature of man and his relation to the world; the second concerns Edwards' uncritical assent to ancient mythologies which were about to be dissolved by the epistemological certainties of the scientific age. We could say that it is unfortunate that he held to the latter, but that it is still possible to distill from them the more durable discoveries in the former division of his thought. According to this interpretation of his belief in God, we could urbanely excuse him for the naive religious exuberances common to his age but strange to ours, and take what remains to prove that he is indeed a modern thinker.

Such an interpretation of Edwards would seriously err. We have already seen that there is unavailable to man any relationship with a being outside the visible finitude of history. Like the philosopher with his beetle Edwards was frequently to insist that there is no private knowledge of God from which other men are excluded. As we observed above[1] all his talk about God would have to do with the way in which men lived with one another. Therefore, however strange his talk about God must seem to the ear of a more sophisticated and less passionate age, it is still the case that he is grounding that talk on experience as available to us as it was to him.

It had once momentarily appeared to Edwards in his adolescence that the existence of God was so obvious it could be proved.[2] Nowhere in his mature thought, however, does he engage himself in a serious attempt at such a proof. In fact, in the most detailed discussion of God's relationship to the world he develops a conception that makes it impossible even to frame an argument for God's existence. Since created substance is contingent, he argued, it must be an effect and therefore have a cause; for being contingent it cannot have itself for its own cause.

> Therefore the existence of created substances, in each successive moment, must be the effect of the immediate agency, will, and power of God. . . . It will certainly follow from these things, that God's *preserving* created things in being is perfectly equivalent to a *continued creation,* or to his creating those things out of nothing at *each moment* of their existence.[3]

[1] See above, p. 44.   [2] See above, p. 66.
[3] *Works* (see Chap. One, note 7), II, 488f.

The God in whom Edwards once longed to be swallowed up is now thrust back into the mystery that lies behind all the eventfulness and factuality of the world. There is no permanence to the things that exist; there is nothing in substance or in the nature of the personality that can guarantee continued existence. Everthing depends on the creative agency of God, even the fact that there are things and persons at all, instead of a patternless, chaotic series of happenings.

> There is no identity or oneness . . . but what depends on the *arbitrary* constitution of the Creator; why by his wise sovereign establishment so unites these successive new effects, that he *treats them as one,* by communicating to them like properties, relations and circumstances; and so leads *us* to regard and treat them as *one.* When I call this an *arbitrary constitution,* I mean, it is a constitution which depends on nothing but the divine will; which divine will depends on nothing but the *divine wisdom.*[4]

There is no explanation of the origin and nature of the world or of the things in it, then, that can come from the world itself. Not even the theory of gravity, as Newton had stated it in Edwards' time, can explain the connectedness of events, since gravity, too, depends on the arbitrary will of God.

The doctrine of *creatio continuo* works a difficult feature into our talking about God. It makes it impossible for us to speak about God with any certainty at all. We might assume that since the universe has been so structured for these several billion years it will continue a while longer. But this is an invalid assumption. According to Edwards, it could cease existing any moment. In an instant all things could pass into chaos, or another universe could be substituted in the place of the present one. Therefore, we have combined in this notion both the impermanence of all existing things and the utter freedom

---

[4] *Works,* II, 490.

of God. It would appear that Edwards has disqualified his own talk about God in this case. Indeed, he once admits himself that all our talk about God is "improper."[5]

Edwards does not cease from talking about God, however, nor does he hesitate to enter into the very being of God to describe his eternal nature. We must determine whether he has built a contradiction into his system—by talking about a God who transcends all our efforts to know him—or whether he has found a way of combining God's utter freedom from the finitude of the world with the finitude of our own knowledge. In a sermon on the sovereignty of God there is a curious statement that intentionally joins both of the terms of this apparent contradiction, thereby suggesting that Edwards was aware of it himself. He asks us to see

> what cause we have to admire the grace of God, that he should condescend to become bound to us by covenant; that he, who is naturally supreme in his dominion over us, who is our absolute proprietor, and may do with us as he pleases, and is under no obligation to us; that he should as it were, relinquish his absolute freedom and should cease to be merely sovereign in his dispensations towards believers, when once they have believed in Christ, and should for their more abundant consolation, become bound. So that they can challenge salvation of this Sovereign; they can demand it through Christ, as a debt. And it would be prejudicial to the glory of God's attributes, to deny it to them; it would be contrary to his justice and faithfulness.[6]

How is it that God's *absolute freedom* is to be reconciled with his *indebtedness* to mere men? The only way we can answer this question is momentarily to suspend our incredulity and to follow Edwards into his discussion of the inner nature of God, i.e., the doctrine of the trinity.

On our way into this examination we must remember that

[5] *Works*, II, 514.   [6] *Works*, IV, 559.

Edwards has already set out some fundamental propositions on the nature of freedom that will affect the outcome of the present discussion. It must be seen, for example, that God's "absolute freedom" cannot be a freedom of self-determination. The reason for this is not that self-determination is a *divine impossibility,* but that it is a *contradictory concept.* It is not that it is impossible for God to be self-determining, but that it is impossible to think of God determining himself; talk about God's self-determination is meaningless; just as talk about man's self-determination is meaningless. Since Edwards does not provide any special categories for the discussion of God's volition, as distinct from man's volition, we must assume that the categories already proposed for man apply to God as well. It is in the doctrine of the trinity that this aspect of God is considered.

Edwards never prepared a work on the trinity for publication, although there were several essays on the subject in his miscellaneous notes. Like most of the documents found in this vast collection, they seem to have been written down at many different times and then usually at great speed. They have been subsequently edited and published under two separate titles.[7] The basic idea on which this doctrine is initiated is that God's will, like man's, is as the most apparent good is. And what can be the most apparent good to God except that which is "infinitely the greatest and best of beings,"[8] which can be nothing but God himself. Therefore, since

> tis common when speaking of the Divine happiness to say that God is Infinitely Happy in the Enjoyment of himself, in Perfectly beholding & Infinitely loving, & Rejoicing in, his own Essence & Perfections . . . it must be supposed that

[7] *Observations Concerning the Scripture Oeconomy of the Trinity and Covenant of Redemption,* ed. Egbert C. Smyth (New York: Charles Scribner's Sons, 1880); *An Unpublished Essay of Edwards on the Trinity,* ed. George Park Fisher (New York: Charles Scribner's Sons, 1903).

[8] *Works,* II, 200.

> God perpetually and Eternally has a most Perfect Idea of himself, as it were an exact Image and Representation of Himself ever before him and in actual view, & from hence arises a most pure and Perfect act or energy in the Godhead, which is the divine Love, Complacence, and Joy.[9]

God's idea of himself is perfect, and, unlike the relations between man and man where one is *in* the image of the other rather than *being* that image itself,[10] we may "suppose the deity to be truly & Properly Repeated by Gods thus having an Idea of himself & that this Idea of God is truly God."[11] The God who is repeated in the image of himself "is the second Person in the Trinity, the Only begotten & dearly beloved Son of G."[12] The second person can then be properly understood as the "Logos of G.," whether "we interpret it of the Reason of G. or of the word of G. If it signifies the Reason & understanding of G., I suppose it wont be denied that tis the same thing with God's Idea."[13] And since God loves that image of himself and since that image loves God, a sacred energy arises between the Father and the Son in mutually loving and delighting in each other.

> The deity becomes all act, the divine essence it self flows out & is as it were breathed forth in Love & Joy. So that the Godhead therein stands forth in yet another manner of subsistence, & there Proceeds the 3d Person in the Trinity, the holy spirit, viz. the Deity in act, for there is no other act but the act of the will.[14]

By now it has become obvious that Edwards is drawing the doctrine of the trinity out into an analogy with his conception of human agency. The Father, or the first person in the trinity, is the agent himself, and just as the agent cannot be imagined apart from his agency and the particular understanding that

---

[9] *An Unpublished Essay* (see note 7), pp. 77f.   [10] *Ibid.*, p. 86.
[11] *Ibid.*, p. 80.   [12] *Ibid.*, p. 85.   [13] *Ibid.*, p. 91.
[14] *Ibid*, p. 94.

shapes it, the Father cannot be imagined apart from the Son and the Holy Spirit.

> The Son is the deity generated by Gods understanding, or having an idea of himself & subsisting in that Idea. The Holy Gh. is the Deity subsisting in act, or the divine essence flowing out and Breathed forth in Gods Infinite love to & delight in himself. & I believe the whole divine Essence does Truly & distinctly subsist both in the divine Idea & divine Love, and that each of them are Properly distinct Persons.[15]

However precisely Edwards might have drawn out the analogy between the trinitarian structure of the being of God and the psychological structure of the being of man, we still do not know why he felt it necessary to say that God was *bound* to man through Christ, and that man could *demand* salvation through Christ as though it were a debt owed man. We must therefore ascertain more specifically toward which end God is determined. If the greatest apparent good for God is his own being as it is reflected in the second person, precisely how are we to understand this with relation to the world? As in our analysis of human volition, now that we know *how* God's will operates we must see *what* he actually wills.

It is this question to which Edwards had turned in his *Dissertation Concerning the End for Which God Created the World,* one of the volumes he wrote in the Indian mission post at Stockbridge. Beginning with the thesis that in the creation of the world God would have had to have himself as his own highest end, he wonders why there should have been a creation at all. He decides that God laid out the earth and the heavens only because his attributes thereby have a more glorious "display" than they would have had if there had never been existence outside God himself. God will emanate his glory just

15 *Ibid.,* p. 110.

as the sun its light, and roots their sap and life.[16] "But," he cautions,

> a disposition to communicate of its life and sap to its fruits, is not so properly the cause of its producing those fruits, as its disposition to communicate itself, or diffuse its sap and life in general. Therefore, to speak more strictly according to truth, we may suppose, *that a disposition in God, as an original property of his nature, to an emanation of his own infinite fulness, was what excited him to create the world; and so that the emanation itself was aimed at by him as a last end of the creation.*[17]

Here we find Edwards reaching back for a metaphor first given systematic use by the pagan philosopher Plotinus, and subsequently mediated into the Christian tradition by Augustine: God as emanating light. It was of the nature of God, Plotinus taught, that he should communicate himself *ad extra,* just as it was of the nature of the sun to communicate its own brilliance to things outside itself. It is sometimes said that Edwards had to be under the influence of the Cambridge Platonists to have used such ideas, but the Puritans were universally fond of this metaphor. There are many possible sources of it for Edwards. What is important to see is that wherever it originated it becomes his own idea when it is brought into his thought, and it is made there to serve the distinctive ends of his theology.

In other places Edwards makes it clear that he does not mean to work out a typically Greek cosmology on the basis of this metaphor, asserting various levels of emanated being, because God's communication of himself

> is really only to intelligent beings. The communication of himself to their understandings is his glory and the commu-

nication of himself with respect to their wills, the enjoying faculty is their happiness.[18]

The emanated light is in a special sense only for those intelligent beings who are not only able to see God "displayed" in the creation, but are able so to respond to his light that God can be said to be their happiness. The important thing about these emanations is not that they occur but that they excite in those beings who receive them what Edwards will call "remanations." As we shall see in greater detail in a subsequent chapter, he was fond of expressing this point in metaphor. Of true saints, united to the Spirit of Christ, he said that

> the light of the Sun of Righteousness don't only shine upon them, but is so communicated to them that they shine also, and become little images of that Sun which shines upon them; the sap of the true vine is not only conveyed into them, as the sap of a tree may be conveyed into a vessel, but is conveyed as sap is from a tree into one of its living branches, where it becomes a principle of life.[19]

In sum, we can say that God's end in creation is not merely the creation, nor is it the establishment of a certain order within the creation, nor is it even the emanation of his glory to lifeless or "darksome" matter; rather *God's last end in creating the world is reached when his moral, intelligent creatures make him their own last end.* "There are many reasons to think that what God has in view, in an increasing communication of himself throughout eternity, is an increasing knowledge of God, love to him, and joy in him."[20]

In Edwards' doctrine of the trinity we learned that God's will, like man's, is as the most apparent good is. In his discussion of God's end in the creation of the world we learned that God has reached his own last end when he has become

[18] *Miscellanies*, Yale MSS., No. 332.
[19] *Religious Affections*, ed. John E. Smith (New Haven, 1959), pp. 200f.
[20] *Works*, II, 210.

the most apparent good for man. It is in the doctrine of the covenant that Edwards brings these two notions together. As a doctrine the covenant had already enjoyed a long tradition by Edwards' time, particularly in Puritan thought. A covenant theology was first enunciated in the work of the Swiss Reformer Oecolampadius. Owing to his influence on the English Protestants during and following the Marian persecutions, the doctrine came to be a prominent piece of Reformed theology. Among its other important appearances, the covenant is used in the Westminster Confession to describe the nature of the relationship between God and man. By the time that document was framed (1642), there had developed what has since been referred to as the "double covenant." According to this scheme there was first a covenant of works established between Adam and God, by which Adam was expected to fulfill certain expectations by good works. Had he done so God would have been obligated to pay him with salvation. But Adam broke the first covenant, and though God was not required by its terms to reconsider, he did nonetheless, and a second was established. This time, however, God did not risk the bestowal of his glorious reward on something so feeble as sinful man; but he both established the covenant and fulfilled it in the man Christ Jesus.

Edwards adopts this scheme from his theological forbears without any important changes. His references to the covenant of works, however, are scant.[21] He is much more concerned with the "eternal covenant" that has to do with "that particular affair of men's redemption."[22] As Edwards weaves it into his thought the covenant comes to comprehend two kinds of relations: between the persons of the trinity, and between God and

[21] The most explicit treatment of the double covenant is found in the "Annotations on Passages of Scripture," *Selections from the Unpublished Writings of Jonathan Edwards, of America,* ed. Alexander B. Grosart (Edinburgh: Ballantyne and Co., 1865), pp. 86f.

[22] Smyth, ed. (see footnote 7), p. 28.

man. As it pertains to the intra-trinitarian relations the covenant recasts the doctrine of the trinity in terms of a contractual agreement and "oeconomy" of action. Since the Father is the one person in the trinity who "is especially injured by sin, and who is therefore the Person whose wrath is enkindled, and whose justice and vengeance are to be executed, and must be satisfied," it is he who chooses the "Person that shall be the Redeemer, and appoints Him."[23] It is first within the trinity that God decides that he must make himself apparent to man —to man for whom God is by no means the most apparent good; indeed, God is an enemy. Therefore, the Son, who is the word or idea of God, will be "spoken" to man; he will appear in the flesh.

The other kind of relation included in the covenant is that between Christ and man. It is by this covenant that Christ—as God made apparent—binds himself to the church. For a covenant to be authentic there must be a condition which upon being filled binds each participant in the covenant to the other. In the so-called covenant of works the condition was Adam's righteousness. But now there is a radical difference in the covenant between God and man, for the condition which validates it has already been fulfilled by Christ; Christ has become our righteousness. The covenant is completed only when Christ's people *close with Him and adhere to Him.*"[24]

This is a delicate point since Edwards must make sure that "closing with Christ," which he elsewhere refers to as "faith," is not itself a kind of work of righteousness. Here he is careful not to say that faith is a condition of the covenant because "making faith a *condition* of life fills the mind with innumerable difficulties about faith and works, and how to distinguish them."[25] The danger is that one might come to think that the covenant between Christ and the soul must be *preceded* by faith if we call faith a condition. But, Edwards insists,

[23] *Ibid.,* p. 29f.   [24] *Ibid.,* p. 68.   [25] *Ibid.,* p. 67.

we can do nothing but only receive Christ and what He has done already. Salvation is not offered to us upon any condition, but freely and for nothing. We are to do nothing for it; we are only to take it. This *taking* and *receiving* is *faith* ... It is very improper to say that a *covenant* is made with men, any otherwise than in Christ; for there is a vast difference between a free offer and a covenant. The covenant was made with Christ, and in Him with His mystical body; and the condition of the covenant is Christ's perfect obedience and sufferings. And that, that is made to men, is a free *offer*.[26]

Here then is why Edwards is able to say that man can *demand* salvation of God as though it were a debt God owed man: by the covenant made within the trinity God has, in effect, committed himself entirely to the Christ made apparent. Since the condition for the covenant between Christ and man has already been satisfied by "Christ's perfect obedience and sufferings," man need close this covenant merely by accepting that which God offers in Christ. Or, in other words, man may lay claim to the salvation of God merely by looking on Christ, merely by "seeing" Christ as his most apparent good. When man so beholds Christ he has *ipso facto* already received the salvation offered by God, for that salvation is nothing other than God's becoming the most apparent good for man.

There is probably no field of investigation within the theological discipline which gives greater cause for ridiculing the academic theologian than the doctrines of the trinity and the covenant. It is comically presumptuous for a man to think that he can mount up on high and know the inner relations and operations of God better even than he can know himself. But in the embrace of a mind as competent as Edwards' the doctrine serves to do just the opposite: instead of transporting the speculative imagination into the hidden recesses of the divine

[26] *Ibid.*, pp. 65f.

nature, it manages to bring the whole mystery of God into the casual impermanence of the world. Edwards intends to make it impossible for us to talk about God as though he were a being somehow apart and independent from the world of our experience. It is because of the doctrine of the trinity that every sentence about God becomes at the same time a sentence which falls within the range of our own understanding. The deity, he said, was all act. Because he used the same categories for God that he used for man, he also taught that every act of the deity was *ad extra*. Just as there are no actions *within* man, independent of his actions in the world, there are no actions *within* the being of God that do not affect the world.

At the same time a cautionary word must be uttered over these reflections. To have said that Edwards' doctrine of the trinity empties God of his privacy and makes of him a God whose nature it is to become visible within the historical experience of man, is not to have said that God is in any sense to be identified as the world or some aspect of it. It is here that we must be reminded of the difficult notion that God is a continuous creator of the world. We cannot therefore argue that God is equivalent, say, to the natural process of evolution by which each organic thing has its own teleology. Edwards' doctrine is not calling for the immanence of God in any usual sense. There is no opening here into a natural theology by which one might be able to proceed from facts in the world to truths about the nature of God. There is nothing about the world in itself that makes God visible. It is only Christ who makes God visible.

VI.

GOD IS AS THE MOST
APPARENT CHRIST IS

Ours is not an age of the knowledge of God. That man is regarded as deluded who expects the divine suddenly to shatter through the limitations of human comprehensibility to make itself an object of knowledge. If there are men who bother to seek out the being of God at all they will likely find themselves reaching the boundaries of their understanding without any clear evidence of what lies beyond in the unknown. If any satisfy themselves that the Unknown is God; if they suppose that it is God that lies somewhere beyond the edge of philosophic probabilities and scientific certainties, it is decidedly not a God whom they could worship or in whom their lives could find purpose and meaning. These seem to be the alternatives for the contemporary reflection: either a God who eludes all our efforts to think of him with anything but passionless notions, or no God at all. It is certainly no surprise that in the light of these alternatives, the figure of Christ, if he is to emerge from his mythological entombment at all, can become for modern man little more than a bloodless example for one or another sentimental ethic.

The thinker whose views of Christ seem to consist best with the contemporary mood is Søren Kierkegaard. Suppose it were true what Christians say, Kierkegaard mused in the pseudonym of Johannes Climacus, that God left the Unknown to become man. It must therefore be the case that he dwelt *incognito* in the man Jesus. Of course, Climacus thought that this was by no means a limitation placed upon God. In his explanation of this point he characteristically diverts his discussion into an allegory. He has us imagine a king who has fallen in love with a humble maiden. How may the king so love the maiden that she will understand his love and therefore love him in return? He could elevate the maiden; he could appear before her in all the splendor of his office and sweep her off breathless to his palace. But such an elevation of the maiden could not result in a relationship of true understanding, the king can see, for he would have caused the maiden to be something she is not. Moreover, the king would have overwhelmed her with his great office and with his power, rather than his love. Therefore, Climacus concludes, the king must *descend* from his lofty majesty. He must empty himself of his great power, and enter fully into the circumstances of the maiden. He must take on the life of a servant who can share genuinely in the life of the maiden, and whom she can understand without being overwhelmed or removed from the normal context of her life. It is, of course, of the greatest importance that the king never reveal his royalty to the maiden, for if the purple of his robes ever once should show through the servant's clothing, the humble maiden would fall into despair for she could see that she had been deceived.

But, at the same time, Kierkegaard did not want us to think that if this were the strategy of God all is thereby solved, for when God became man in order that man might understand God and God understand man, man is confronted with the final unanswerable question: how do I know that this man is God? "There lives an individual," Climacus says,

> whose appearance is precisely like that of other men; he grows up to manhood like others, he marries, he has an

occupation by which he earns his livelihood, and he makes provision for the future as befits a man. . . . This man is also God. How do I know? I cannot know it, for in order to know it I would have to know God, and the nature of the difference between God and man; and this I cannot know. . . .[1]

This is what Kierkegaard called the "absolute paradox," for it is the act of God—who is absolutely unlike man—to become absolutely like man. How then can man understand the absolutely unlike which has become the absolutely like? As is well known, Kierkegaard is not without an answer to this final question. In subsequent writings he calls man to an intense subject-ness; he asks that man seize upon the objective uncertainty that Christ was God and appropriate it unto himself by an act of the most passionate inwardness.

Although Edwards' words, especially as we compare them to the great Danish ironist's, have about them the dullness of the pedant, he is in fundamental agreement with Kierkegaard and the entire classical Christian tradition that, whatever is to be said of the divinity of Christ, he is fully human. He is "like us in every respect," the Fathers said at Chalcedon in 451. Edwards accepted the judgment of the Christian tradition that Christ's work of redemption required his full humanity.

Though Christ, as God, was infinitely sufficient for the work, yet to his being in an immediate capacity for it, it was needful that he should not only be God, but man. If Christ had remained only in the divine nature, he would not have been in a capacity to have purchased our salvation; not from any imperfection of the divine nature, but by reason of its absolute and infinite perfection: *for Christ, merely as God, was not capable either of that obedience or suffering that was needed.* The divine nature is not capable

[1] *Philosophical Fragments or a Fragment of Philosophy,* trans. David F. Swenson (Princeton, 1936), p. 36.

of suffering; for it is infinitely above all suffering. Neither
is it capable of obedience to that law that was given to man.
It is as impossible that one who is only God should obey
the law that was given to man, as it is that he should suffer
man's punishment.[2]

Whatever salvation consists in, its accomplishment requires
Christ to be obedient and to suffer. These are exclusively human categories. Whatever God must do to save man, he must
do it strictly within the dimensions of man's historical nature.
More precisely, he must do it within the dimensions of the
history of one particular person.

As nothing was done before Christ's incarnation, so nothing
was done after his resurrection, to purchase redemption for
men. Nor will there ever be any thing more done to all
eternity. But that very moment that the human nature of
Christ ceased to remain under the power of death, the ut-
most farthing was paid of the price of the salvation of every
one of the elect.[3]

Up to this point Edwards' thought is predictably orthodox
and commonplace, but from now on his thinking about the
nature of Christ begins to acquire its own distinctiveness. The
final shape of his christology has almost nothing in common
with either Kierkegaard or the orthodox Protestant theologians.
In sharp contrast to Kierkegaard, Edwards will not send men
into their own inwardness. We have already had abundant
evidence that this would be impossible given his philosophic
presuppositions. In fact, we can see that quite another resolution of the unanswerable question—how do we know that
this man is God?—is required. We can see that the answer
will not have to do with what a man does with his subjectivity,
but what a man views with his understanding and subsequently

[2] "History of the Work of Redemption," *Works* (see Chap. One, note 7),
I, 396. Italics mine.
[3] *Ibid.*

responds to with his will. We have seen in previous chapters that the only way God is able to influence a man is not by some invisible, internal influence, but by becoming man's reason for doing what he does. Edwards' God, unlike Kierkegaard's, cannot dwell *incognito* in Christ; if he is to become God at all he must become man's most apparent good. Edwards' christology, therefore, is his attempt to bring men around to see the God-man Christ as their greatest good.

This overall christological design causes Edwards to make a radical departure from the traditional orthodox discussion of the nature of Christ as well. From the time of the Reformation there had been developing a large and elaborate collection of doctrines concerning the person, work and states of Christ, originating principally in the bitter altercations between the Lutheran and Reformed divines over various points in the understanding of Christ. These disputes were kept alive well into the 19th century, and in some cases into the 20th. It is therefore a matter of considerable interest that Edwards can move straight through this theological snake pit of uncharitable attack and counterattack without paying the least attention to what is going on in it. This is all the more striking if we consider that this material was well-known to him. He had read widely in the weightiest volumes of the orthodox divines of the seventeenth and eighteenth centuries. But the problem of the *unio personalis,* or the *communicatio idiomatum,* or even the characteristically Reformed debate over what was called the "extra-Calvinisticum" and the repeated affirmation that the finite was not capable of assuming attributes of the divine (*finitum non capax infinitum*), appear either not at all in Edwards' work, or they are dealt with so cursorily that we must conclude that he had no interest in them. The reason for the omission of such large quantities of traditional material can only be that Edwards thought it irrelevant to the major christological task as he understood it. If one should wonder how our understanding of the man Christ is at the same time an understanding of God, his curiosity would not have been properly answered by the traditional methods of dealing conceptually with the nature of Christ. Edwards was certain that a thorough knowledge of, say, the doctrine of the *statu exinanitionis* would hardly capture the heart.

Therefore, the Christ who emerges in the pages of Edwards' sermons and essays is a Christ who brilliantly *appears* to the view of man. He is a Christ who is like us in every respect—and yet by the character of his humanity he moves us to conduct our lives in a radical new way. Since Edwards cannot cause the divinity of Christ to appear to us through any transhistorical method or through the orthodox metaphysical categories, he must cause Christ to become our most apparent good through historical categories. His Christ is not one we are to think about, his is a Christ we are to see. Edwards does not want to teach us a doctrine about Christ, he wants to make Christ a fact that has great force in our lives. Therefore, one often has the impression that he is painting a verbal picture of Christ. The metaphors translate easily into visible components. Our attention is arrested by the frequent use of contrast, color and movement. We become increasingly aware, as we observe Edwards at work on his portrait, that there is nothing more to Christ than what we can be led to see. The edges of the canvas are the historical limitations under which every human being must pursue life and wisdom. He does not try by means of his art to direct us to something that cannot be said or shown. We are ever reminded that Christ must be seen to be Christ. What cannot be seen is spiritually irrelevant.

The first strokes of his intellectual brush are broad dark movements that literally fill the canvas. Exposing a woefully inadequate knowledge of history Edwards understands the time of the birth of Christ to be a time of great war and strife. God intentionally waited for this to happen before becoming incarnate, because "it pleased God that the curse should once, before the restoration by Christ, be executed in a universal destruction, as it were, of the very form of earth, that the dire effects of the fall might once in such a way be seen before the recovery of Christ."[4] Against this rule of darkness and universal destruction, we must paint the birth of Christ. But the darkness of the background is overwhelming. We can scarcely see Christ simply because of the insignificant circumstances of his birth. He was born to a poor virgin who was espoused to a poor man, both of whom were of the now broken house of David; so he was "born in a very low condition, even in a stable, and laid in a manger."[5] From the beginning Christ was bound to suffer; he was bound to be painted with the same dark hues with which the world was represented. He was bound to be the innocent and helpless victim of the world's evils. "He was born to that end that he might die; and therefore he did as it were begin to die as soon as he was born. . . . He suffered in his birth, as though he had been meaner and viler than a man, and not possessed of the dignity of human nature, but had been of the rank of the brute creatures."[6] Then in his life as a carpenter, a "servile and obscure life, in a mean laborious occupation," he was the subject of a humiliation that "in some respects was greater in his private life than in the time of his public ministry."[7] The first thirty years of his life

> he spent among mean ordinary men, as it were in silence, without those manifestations of his glory, or any thing to make him to be taken notice of more than any ordinary mechanic, but only the spotless purity and eminent holiness of his life; and that was in great measure hid in obscurity; so that he was little taken notice of till after his baptism.[8]

The crude stiff brush with which the universal destruction of the background was painted, has been used for Christ's birth and his first thirty years as well. Thus far there is no contrast;

[4] *Works,* I, 397.   [5] *Works,* I, 399.   [6] *Works,* I, 412.
[7] *Works,* I, 413.   [8] *Ibid.*

there is only the suffering which comes from his full sharing in the suffering of all men.

But his baptism by no means brings an end to this suffering. If there is any more visibility of Christ it is possibly because he now suffers more than others; he now begins to take the center of the canvas of night. In his public life, from the time of "his baptism till the night wherein he was betrayed," he began to suffer from the particular ill intentions of men.

> He was despised and rejected of men. He was by most esteemed a poor, insignificant person; one of little account, slighted for his low parentage, and his mean city Nazareth.
> . . . They wished him dead, and were continually seeking to murder him; sometimes by force, and sometimes by craft.
> . . . He was thus hated and reproached by his own visible people.[9]

It is in the last moments of his public ministry, "from the evening of the night on which he was betrayed to his resurrection," that he underwent his "greatest humiliation and suffering, by which he principally made satisfaction to the justice of God for the sins of men." When Edwards paints this scene onto the raging shapes of his canvas it seems as though he wants us to see that of all the instances of suffering this is the most representative; it is in this one moment of evil that all the world's evil is summarized.

> In those days crucifixion was the most tormenting kind of death by which any were wont to be executed. There was no death wherein the person expired so much of mere torment: and hence the Roman word which signifies *torment*, is taken from this kind of death. And besides what our Lord endured in this excruciating death in his body, he endured vastly more in his soul. Now was that travail of his soul, of which we read in the prophet; now it pleased

9 *Works,* I, 413f.

God to bruise him, and to put him to grief; now he poured out his soul unto death, as in Isa. Iiii.[10]

Suffering is passive. Christ in his suffering is the innocent victim of the world's savagery. Edwards thought that his suffering was consequently of the design of God, not because God was evil himself but because the ethical structure of the universe calls for a system of rewards and punishments and therefore the evil of man must be punished. It is Christ who suffers the punishment for man's sins. Of course, this notion is not new with Edwards, since from the time of the Bible Christ has been understood as the paschal lamb whose sacrifice takes away the sins of the world. But while the concept is ancient, Edwards makes a new use of it. It was Anselm in the eleventh century who had proposed the most enduring manner of using the metaphor of the sacrificial death of Christ. In the *Cur Deus Homo* Anselm brings Boso, his imaginary interlocutor, through a discussion of the heinousness of sin against the person of Christ. Boso concludes with the remark, "A sin committed upon his person exceeds beyond comparison all the sins which can be thought of, that do not affect his person." "You say well," Anselm replies, "and hence we see that no enormity or multitude of sins, apart from the Divine person, can for a moment be compared with a bodily injury, afflicted on that man."[11] In Anselm's hands the sacrifice is understood in quantitative terms. Since a single sin against the person of Christ far exceeds the total of all the other sins of man, and since Christ will give his own life voluntarily, he will give to God that which is greater than all the offense ever made by man against God; Christ's death satisfies God's justice arithmetically.

There is no talk of quantity in Edwards' understanding of

10 *Works*, I, 415f.
11 *Saint Anselm: Basic Writings*, trans. S. N. Deane (La Salle, 1962), pp. 262f.

Christ's suffering. Edwards' Christ is primarily visual; his suffering amounts to nothing unless it is seen. Anselm's Christ could have suffered in total invisibility, since the point of his suffering was the quantitative satisfaction of God's justice. Edwards is not really talking about the supra-historical communications between Christ and God; he is painting a canvas by which he intends powerfully to command our attention. He does not want to find some comfortable resolution of the intellectually puzzling conflict of justice and mercy in God; he wants our eye, and with that our heart. It is to the excellency, or the beauty, of Christ that he has committed his art. The aesthetic principles of this portraiture are contrast and proportionality. Thus far the contrasts consist in the fragile brilliance of Christ's purity set over against the ragged darkness of evil. By his innocence the very scope of evil is revealed. But the canvas also evidences a striking proportionality. It is not just that the light and darkness are set in contrast; for the light, we find, is at the center of the canvas. Christ is at the center of evil. All of the cruelty of this world stands in sharp contrast not simply to a general sort of good, but to the person of Christ. Christ's innocence is the very definition of evil. Edwards is saying that to look at Christ is to see the nature and the range of the world's imperfections. It is to see the pain and indignity and death that empties life of its meaning.

If this is the manner of depicting Christ's suffering, how then are we to see his obedience? We are surprised to learn that it "was by the same things that Christ hath satisfied God's justice, and also purchased eternal happiness. This satisfaction and purchase of Christ were not only both carried on through the whole time of Christ's humiliation, but they were both carried on by the same things."[12] Nothing new is added to the canvas; those things by which Edwards signified his suffering also signify his obedience. How is this the case? The purity of Christ, the

12 *Works*, I, 403.

source of his innocence, is his righteousness by the moral law. There was simply no violation of the ten commandments.[13] But this kind of obedience cannot count very much, for this was all that was expected of Adam under the covenant of works, and it was over this kind of obedience that the darkness of evil triumphed. Edwards adds an interesting new category to this discussion: there is a new kind of law, "the mediatorial law," under which Christ has been placed.

> As that act of disobedience by which we fell, was dis-obedience to a positive precept that Christ never was under, viz., that of abstaining from the tree of knowledge of good and evil; so that act of obedience by which principally we are redeemed, is obedience to a positive precept that Adam never was under, viz., the precept of laying down his life.[14]

While this adds nothing new to his canvas, it provides us with a strikingly new manner of viewing the suffering of Christ. Now, instead of seeing his death as the victimization of an innocent because of his passive defenselessness, we see in it a dramatic intentionality. The purity of Christ is not the last feeble flash of light about to be extinguished by the eternal night, but a bold new attack against the darkness. Suddenly the pattern of the canvas reverses itself; when we see that the suffering of Christ is really a new kind of obedience, then we can see that it is the darkness and not the light that is about to be vanquished.

Now all of the acts of Christ's life can be described according to the light which they shed into the world. The most important description

> of the acts by which Christ purchased redemption, regards *the virtues that Christ exercised and manifested in them.* And here I would observe, that Christ in doing the work

13 *Works,* I, 404f.
14 "Justification by Faith Alone," *Works,* IV, 99.

that he had to do here in the world for our redemption, exercised every possible virtue and grace. . . . Every virtue in him was perfect. Virtue itself was greater in him than in any other; and it was under greater advantages to shine in him than in any other. Strict virtue shines most when most tried: but never any virtue had such trials as Christ's had.[15]

We can do little here to improve on the artfulness with which Edwards executes this aspect of his "apparent" Christ. In addition to the virtues he exercised toward God and toward himself, such as humility, patience, and contempt of the world,

Christ, in the work which he wrought out, in a wonderful manner exercised those *virtues which more immediately respect other men*. And these may be summed up under two heads, viz., meakness and love.

Christ's meakness was his humble calmness of spirit under the provocations that he met with. . . . If we consider how much he was hated, what abuses he suffered from the vilest of men, how great his sufferings from men were, and how spiteful and how contemptuous they were, in offering him these abuses; and also consider how causeless and unreasonable these abuses were, how undeserving he was of them, and how much deserving of the contrary, viz., of love, and honor, and good treatment at their hands: I say, if we consider these things, no man ever met with a thousandth part of the provocation that Christ met with from men: and yet how meek was he under all! How composed and quiet his spirit.[16]

And never did there appear such an instance of love to men. Christ's love to men that he showed on earth, and especially in going through his last sufferings, and offering up his life and soul under those sufferings, which was his greatest act of love, was far beyond all parallel.[17]

[15] "History of Redemption," *Works,* I, 409f.
[16] *Works,* I, 411.   [17] *Works,* I, 412.

If the significant aspect of Christ's suffering is that it *appears* to men, the significance of his positive obedience, or righteousness, is that it is an *apparent righteousness*. Edwards is not concerned with the fact that Christ loved, but rather with the way that it "showed on earth," such that never before "did there *appear* such an instance of love to men." Christ's virtues were said to *"shine"* in him more than in any other; the virtues which he exercised in respect to God *"appeared* in Christ in the work that he did for our redemption;" the virtues respecting himself "he most wonderfully *manifested*."[18]

The canvas before which we have put ourselves in this chapter was by no means a casual work of Edwards. Indeed, we might so regard his life and thought that this great portrait of Christ can be seen as the absolute center of his life work. The visual brilliance of Christ is a theme that is found repeatedly through his writing and preaching. He was especially fond of interpreting the biblical material in this fashion. In one of his finest sermons, "The Excellency of Christ," delivered in Northampton in 1734, during the most rewarding period of his ministry, the text is taken from Revelation 5:5f., in which there occur the metaphors of the lion and the lamb. With the freedom of interpretation this particular book of scripture invites, he says that these two metaphors are applicable to Christ. Thus he proposes as the doctrine for this discourse that "there is an admirable conjunction of diverse excellencies in Jesus Christ."

> The lion and the lamb, though very diverse kinds of creatures, yet have each their peculiar excellencies. The lion excels in strength, and in the majesty of his voice: the lamb excels in meekness and patience, besides the excellent nature of the creature as good for food, and yielding that which is fit for our clothing, and being suitable to be offered in sacrifice to God. But we see that Christ is in the text com-

[18] *Works*, I, 410. Italics mine.

pared to both; because the diverse excellencies of both wonderfully meet in him.[19]

It should be noted in passing that Edwards has come to a
place in his thought that bears a curious similarity to the traditional discussion of the problem of the relationship between
the human and the divine natures in the person of Christ. As
we noted above, he is certainly well-instructed in the classical
and orthodox formulations of this relationship, but now we
can see how he is much more concerned to state it in terms
that will strike the eye and the heart.

> Christ, as he is God, is infinitely great and high above all.
> He is higher than the kings of the earth: for he is King
> of kings and Lord of lords. He is higher than the highest
> angels of heaven. . . . And yet he is one of infinite con-
> descension. . . . His condescension is sufficient to take a
> gracious notice of the most unworthy, sinful creatures, those
> that have infinite ill deservings. . . . it is great enough to
> take their nature upon him, to become one of them, that
> he may be one with them: yea, it is great enough to abase
> himself yet lower for them, even to expose himself to
> shame and spitting; yea, to yield up himself to an igno-
> minious death for them. And what act of condescension can
> be conceived of greater?[20]

Standing before us now is the poet, not the theologian. Edwards in these pages becomes a singer whose art is given wholly
to the attempt to make his hero ours.

> It is he that is terrible out of his holy places; who is might-
> ier than the noise of many waters, yea than the mighty
> waves of the sea; before whom a fire goeth, and burneth up
> his enemies round about. . . . And yet he was the most mar-
> velous instance of meekness, and humble quietness of spirit,
> that ever was; . . . Thus was Christ a lion in majesty, and
> a lamb in slaughter.[21]

[19] *Works*, IV, 180.   [20] *Works*, IV, 180.
[21] *Works*, IV, 183.

There are numerous entries in the *Miscellanies* that deal with this feature of Christ's death. In one, after repeating that his dying upon the cross was the most "wonderfull act of love that ever was," he goes on to say that "the posture that he died in, was very suitable to signifie his free and great [love] he died with his arms spread open as being ready to embrace all that would come to him."[22]

This aspect of Christ's obedience is directly dealt with in a remarkable but rarely studied essay, "Concerning the Necessity and Reasonableness of the Christian Doctrine of Satisfaction for Sin." The usual way of conceiving the doctrine of satisfaction, as we suggested above, was according to the Anselmic *quid pro quo*. Edwards begins his own discussion with a series of reflections that would seem to be taken straight from Anselm. "Justice requires that sin be punished," he says plainly, "because sin deserves judgment."[23] Since sin against God is no small matter, the judgment it deserves is infinite. But no human being can "balance the desert," because whatever repentance or sorrow he might offer for it would fall infinitely short of that which is required. Should God then forgive men without adequate satisfaction? No, Edwards replies, for then chaos is brought into the moral life.[24] So far he argues the case in all its Anselmic purity, but at this point the similarity to Anselm ends. Anselm had to invent a non-historical happening between the Father and the Son in which the exchange of merits was made. To avoid this necessity himself Edwards shifts the metaphor from that of the *quantitative debt* to that of the *sacrificial friend*. He then outlines a small drama of relationships according to this metaphor that illustrates what he thinks is the true doctrine of satisfaction.

Imagine that you have a friend who is dependent upon you for all his good, and that one day this friend begins to abuse

[22] *Miscellanies*, Yale MSS., No. 304.   [23] *Works*, I, 582.
[24] *Works*, I, 588.

you without restraint. Edwards is certain that you would seek to punish him appropriately for his actions, especially in the light of the fact that he should be grateful to you. Now imagine that a third person enters the picture, a very dear friend of yours, and intercedes for the man who has abused you. You would be moved to forgiveness out of your affection for your friend, and all the more so if your friend

> puts himself in the place of that offender, undertaking to appear for him, to represent him, and act in his stead by an exceeding great change in his circumstances, clothes himself with the form of the offender, goes where he is, takes his place in the universe, puts himself into his circumstances, and is in all things made like unto him. . . .[25]

This is as much as to say that your friend has so embraced your offender that you look on the two of them as one, although you are not likely to forgive your offender, Edwards believes, until one more requirement is satisfied,

> which is this, that seeing the offender is an intelligent being, capable of act and choice, he should therefore actively and cordially occur in the affair; that the union between the friend and him should be mutual; that as the friend's heart is united to the offender, so the offender's heart should be united to the friend.[26]

When this has happened then the merit which you know your friend possesses you impute to your offender. You therefore do not forgive him without regard for the law, since the law requires that a person merit what he receives, and pay for what he owes. The offender merits his forgiveness because by his own ethical choice he has returned the love of the friend.

---

[25] *Works,* I, 598. In this and the following passage I have, for the sake of clarity and brevity, substituted the words "friend" and "offender" for "patron" and "client." According to the special sense with which Edwards uses the latter words in this discussion they are identical in meaning to the former.

[26] *Works,* I, 601.

That Edwards is still dealing with what we referred to above as Christ's "apparent righteousness" is made clear in his definition of "merit." "*By merit*," he writes, "I mean any thing whatsoever in any person or being, or about him or belonging to him, which appearing in the view of another is a recommendation of him to that other's regard, esteem or affection." He is simply not concerned to discuss in this context "whether that which thus recommends be real merit, or something that truly, according to the nature of things, is worthy to induce esteem, &c.; but only what actually recommends and appears worthy in the eye of him to whom it recommends the other."[27] This is another expression of Edwards' relativism. He is quite sure there is no way of going back to the *real Christ*, as though there were somehow available to the inquiring mind a *res in facto posita* on which clear and certain knowledge could rest. Indeed, the real Christ is not there anyway. The only Christ there is, is the Christ who appears to us by means of his dramatic assumption of our circumstances. If there is any sense in which Christ is real it is only that in which we have become one with the apparent Christ, when his merits are imputed to us and we are as Christ in the world.

With this we are introduced to another aspect of our portrait of Jonathan Edwards. "The silk-worm is a remarkeable type of Christ," he wrote once in his private notes,

> which when it dies yields us that of which we make such glorious clothing. Christ became a worm for our sakes, and by his death kindled that righteousness with which believers are clothed, and thereby procured that we should be clothed with robes of glory.[28]

So far what we have seen is that Edwards, when he came to his doctrine of Christ's person and work, executed a great

27 *Works,* I, 595.
28 *Images or Shadows of Divine Things,* ed. Perry Miller (New Haven, 1948), No. 35.

canvas in which evil struggled with the good. First we saw that the innocence and purity of Christ set the evil of the world in sharp profile; we could see it for what it was. But then, as almost by an optical trick, we are caused to see that the flashing brilliance of Christ was not overcome by the world but is now overcoming the world. Edwards wanted so to paint his canvas of Christ that we would be astonished by it. He wanted it to capture our hearts, in order that the drama of Christ in the world might be repeated in our own lives; in order that we might be clothed, as he said, with the glorious clothing of Christ.

The reader will recall that we initiated this discussion with the question as to how far Edwards could succeed in both affirming the divinity of Christ and yet describing that divinity in terms that did not take us out of the frame of the historical. The following passage is the clearest statement Edwards will ever make concerning this distinctive aspect of his doctrine of Christ.

> Though his human excellencies are but communications and reflections of his divine; and though this light, as reflected, falls infinitely short of the divine fountain of light in its immediate glory; yet the reflection shines not without its proper advantages, as presented to our view and affection. As the glory of Christ appears in the qualifications of his human nature, it appears to us in excellencies that are of our own kind, that are exercised in our own way and manner, and so, in some respects, are peculiarly fitted to invite our acquaintance and draw our affection. The glory of Christ, as it appears in his divinity, though it be far brighter, yet doth it also more dazzle our eyes, and exceeds the strength or comprehension of our sight: but as it shines in the human excellencies of Christ, it is brought more to a level with our conceptions, and suitableness to our nature and manner, yet retaining a semblance of the same divine beauty, and savor of the same divine sweetness. But

as both divine and human excellencies meet together in Christ, they set off and recommend each other to us.[29]

Having been placed before the canvas of Christ's suffering and obedience, there is nothing outside what we see on that canvas that can cause us to conclude that the person of Christ is divine. There is no private communication from the divine itself; no infallible authority by which such knowledge can be attained. Edwards, we can never forget, lived in a world of unboxed beetles; he was the preacher of the visibility of God. It was an early conclusion of this present study that Edwards saw the only means by which God can ever influence the believer is by becoming his most apparent good. Edwards is convinced that it is in Christ that God attempts so to appear to us.

VII.

SATAN'S ORTHODOXY
AND THE REMANATION
OF THE SAINTS

In his 1731 address in Boston Edwards drew a distinction between the "objective good" and the "inherent good." By the objective good he meant the apparent Christ; he meant the vast imagined canvas we examined in the previous chapter. By the inherent good he was referring to the action of the soul in viewing Christ. The inherent good is of the beholder; the objective good of the beheld. As we studied the objective good, or Christ as the most apparent good, we must now study the inherent good, or the soul of the man for whom Christ is the most apparent good.

There is a certain hazard in making this distinction, since in making it we are the more inclined to think that we are dealing with two separate entities—as separate as a canvas and its viewer. It is the charm and the power of Edwards' thought that this distinction cannot so be drawn that the beholder and the beheld are made independent of each other. We have several times been at some pains to elucidate this same point in other contexts. We have said that the influence of God on the soul, for example, is not to be conceived in the natural terms of cause and effect. God can influence the soul, we found, only when he becomes the soul's reason for doing whatever it does. In the distinction between the inherent and the objective good we are, in essence, describing the same human situation—God's being our most apparent good—from two perspectives: first from the way in which Edwards conceives God's attempt to become our most apparent good through Christ, and subsequently from the way in which we perceive God as our most apparent good.

In more traditional terminology what we are about in this chapter is the study of Edwards' doctrine of faith. By the time he came to this subject the Reformation lay nearly two centuries in the past and the controversies that thrust faith into doctrinal prominence in the sixteenth century had cooled and been largely forgotten in the eighteenth. Therefore, we should be forewarned that when we enter upon this study we are upon ground very different from that which Luther and Calvin had cleared in their passionate warfare with Rome. In a series of sermons preached in 1734 and published under the title, "Justification by Faith Alone," Edwards said that anyone who would allow that the relation between Christ and the believer is one in which the two become one, would also allow

> that there may be something that the true Christian does on his part, whereby he is active in coming into this relation or union, some [act] of the soul of the Christian, that is the Christian's uniting act, or that which is done towards this union or relation (or whatever any please to call it) on the Christian's part: now faith I suppose to be this act.[1]

When Edwards identifies faith as the action of the soul he does so with much more boldness than the Reformers would have dared, since they were concerned to set themselves off against what they considered to be the "works righteousness" preached by the papists. In Calvin's definition of faith, with

---

[1] *Works,* (see Chap. One, note 7), IV, 71.

which Edwards was doubtless familiar, the emphasis falls on quite another place. "Now we shall possess a right definition of faith," Calvin wrote,

> if we call it a firm and certain knowledge of God's benevolence towards us, founded upon the truth of the freely given promise in Christ, both revealed to our minds and sealed upon our hearts through the Holy Spirit.[2]

There is no action of the soul in this definition. Even knowledge here reads as though it were not something the soul *does*, but something it *has*; it is not an act of the mind, but the content of the mind, and in this case a content which is given to the mind.

Of course, none of the Reformers, and Calvin least of all, meant to hold the faithful soul to a state of permanent inactivity. They were only concerned that it was God and not the believer who took the first step in effecting man's salvation. In order to sustain both the action of God and the action of the redeemed man the Reformers drew a sharp distinction between justification and sanctification. Justification was the legal act of God, by which man is declared righteous solely by what Christ had done for him in his suffering and obedience. Sanctification was the subjective, human response to God's objective *extra nos* act of justification. When the Reformers insisted that justification was by faith alone (*sola fide*) they were not giving the power of salvation to faith, but they were emptying faith of its works. They were reducing it to mere receptivity. The sanctification, or love, that followed was therefore not the cause of salvation, but the result of it. But even then sanctification was not exclusively of the saint's own doing. Calvin referred to justification and sanctification together as a *duplex gratia*.[3]

The Reformers had strong reasons for holding to this view

[2] *Institutes of the Christian Religion,* ed. John T. McNeill, trans. Ford Lewis Battles (2 vols.; Philadelphia, 1960), III, ii, 7.

[3] *Ibid.,* III, xi, 1.

of faith. In addition to overthrowing the casuistry of works righteousness, it also provided them with a weapon with which to war against the immense power of the ecclesiastical authorities needed to regulate and determine the efficacy of the various works. But, nonetheless, there was an inconsistency in the very center of the Protestant doctrine of faith. The Reformers did not want to say that man could be saved by his own actions, but they did want to say that his salvation necessitated action. The reason that full clarity was unavailable to the sixteenth century authors of this doctrine is that they were in the habit of using the concept of cause according to its naturalistic understanding. Calvin repeatedly talks about the action of God on the soul as though it were the action of an instrument striking a passive object. The knowledge necessary to salvation is "sealed upon our hearts by the Holy Spirit." And the object which is thus struck is at the same time acting of its own agency. The confusion which arises out of this sort of talk about causation was circumvented by Edwards when he threw out the possibility of talking about the soul in terms of natural causality.[4] What the soul does it can do only for its own reasons —not because it was "violently actuated from without." God, Edwards believed,

> treats men as reasonable creatures, capable of act and choice; and hence sees it fit that they only that are one with Christ by their own act, should be looked upon as one in law. What is real in the union between Christ and his people, is the foundation of what is legal; that is, it is the something that is really in them, and between them, uniting them, that is the ground of the suitableness of their being accounted as one by the Judge.[5]

When we talk of faith, then, or the "inherent good," we are not talking about an inactive soul, nor are we talking about

4 See below, pp. 55ff.
5 "Justification by Faith Alone," *Works*, IV, 71.

an event outside the soul that results in the mechanical prod-
ding of the soul into action. We are talking about something
that is *really there*, uniting the soul to Christ. We must therefore inquire into what Edwards means by the "something"
that is "real" in the union of the believer with Christ.

After his death there was found in Edwards' unpublished
manuscripts a portfolio of miscellaneous remarks on the nature
of faith which he had written down over a long period of time
and according to no particular order. These were subsequently
printed under the title, "Observations on Faith." Only once in
this material does it seem as though he is willing to settle
on a single definition.

> Upon the whole, the best and clearest, and most perfect
> definition of justifying faith, and most according to the
> Scriptures, that I can think of, is this, faith is the soul's
> entirely embracing the revelation of Jesus Christ as our
> Saviour.[6]

Edwards gave more action to the soul than Calvin did, but both
of them in their initial definitions saw that the object of faith
was knowledge. There is no question that the knowledge sealed
on the heart by the Holy Spirit was for Calvin a knowledge
found in scripture. And when Edwards speaks of "revelation"
he too is concerned that we understand this revelation to originate in the words of scripture. There were before Edwards'
reflection numerous examples of spiritual excess that came
from the failure to connect revelation and scripture. In the
confusion of the Great Awakening he saw that one of its most
destructive factors was the notion some of the saints were
under that they were subjects of immediate revelation from
heaven. From bitter experience Edwards the preacher was to
learn what Edwards the young philosopher could have guessed:

> This error will defend and support all errors. As long as a
> person has a notion that he is guided by immediate direc-

---
[6] *Works,* II, 606.

tion from heaven, it makes him incorrigible and impregnable in all his misconduct: for what signifies it, for poor, blind worms of the dust, to go argue with a man, and endeavor to convince him and correct him, that is guided by the immediate counsels and commands of the great Jehovah?[7]

Edwards cannot, however, conclude his investigation into the nature of faith at this point, for he can see that there are serious limitations to his definition. "It may be objected," he observes,

> that this seems to make the revelation more the object of the essential act of faith than Christ. I answer, no; for the revelation is no otherwise the object by this definition, than as it brings and exhibits Christ to us. It is embracing the revelation in a sense and conviction of the goodness and reality of the Saviour it exhibits.[8]

How then shall we distinguish between that knowledge which is of scripture merely, and that which is of scripture insofar as it exhibits Christ?

The very least that can be said is that our knowledge must be *correct*. "If our doctrines concerning him, concerning his divinity, for instance, are false, we have not respect for the Christ of whom the Scriptures speak, but for an imaginary person, infinitely diverse."[9] But this is little more than to say that whatever knowledge of Christ we might have, it must agree with scripture. This is an understanding of knowledge that has serious limitations to it, for this presupposes that knowledge is a *content* of the mind, a collection of propositions or perceptions the truth of which is to be determined by their correspondence to things that lie outside the mind. If Edwards is truly regarding knowledge to be of such a character then he has lost the exhilarating views of the mind and its

---

[7] "Thoughts on Revival," *Works*, III, 365.
[8] "Observation on Faith," *Works*, II, 611f.
[9] "Mysteries of Scripture," *Works*, III, 541.

operations which he had developed as a student at Yale. But, we find, this is not the case. He is acutely aware of the limitations of this sort of knowledge. In fact, it becomes the subject of one of his most memorable sermons, "True Grace Distinguished from the Experience of Devils."

"Nothing in the mind of man," Edwards pronounces in this sermon, "that is of the same nature with what the devils experience, or are the subjects of, is any sure sign of saving grace."[10] Since the devil has the natural understanding of an angel he is capable of great speculative knowledge of the things of God, of the eternal and invisible world. In fact, he probably saw the face of God before the Fall. "And sin has no tendency to destroy the memory." The devil, Edwards explains, "was educated in the best divinity school of the universe, viz., the heaven of heavens."[11] Much of what we know only by doctrine he knows by direct observation. He saw the creation. He knew Christ. The devil is therefore "orthodox in his faith; he believes the true scheme of doctrine; he is no Deist, Socinian, Arian, Pelagian, or Antinomian; the articles of his faith are all sound."[12] Although the *correctness* of one's knowledge of divine things is necessary, it is not correctness alone that is saving, for the knowledge which devils have is both correct and complete. What then is it about knowledge that is saving?

Shall we say that a man has believed properly when he has been deeply moved by what he knows of divine things? No, Edwards believes, for the devils are not left unmoved by what they see of hell; inasmuch as their souls are perfectly intact, they are moved to terror by what they see just as any other rational being is moved to terror by the sight of hell.[13] And it is quite possible, on the other hand, that "persons who have no grace may have great apprehension of an external glory in things heavenly and divine."[14] They will be affected by the

[10] *Works*, IV, 451.   [11] *Works*, IV, 455.   [12] *Works*, IV, 457.
[13] *Works*, IV, 458.   [14] *Works*, IV, 462.

splendid features of heaven or anything external belonging to Jesus Christ, either in his humble state "with blood dripping down," or in his glorified state, therefore "these things are no certain signs of grace."[15]

There is in this quarter of Edwards' thought a certain uneasiness about the usefulness of historical biblical scholarship. Like Kierkegaard in his investigation into the case of the "disciple at second hand," Edwards knows that the mere accumulation of historical knowledge in itself is without gracious result. Of those who rest their faith on such knowledge, he says, "After all that learned men have said to them, there will remain innumerable doubts on their minds: they will be ready, when pinched with some great trial of their faith, to say, How do I know this, or that? How do I know when these histories were written?"[16] It was for the greatest scholar of his generation and a tutor of Indian children to say that

> the gospel was not given only for learned men. There are at least nineteen in twenty, if not ninety-nine in an hundred, of those for whom the Scriptures were written, that are not capable of any certain or effectual conviction of the divine authority of the Scriptures, by such arguments as learned men make use of. . . . Miserable is the condition of the Houssatunnuck Indians, and others, who have lately manifested a desire to be instructed in Christianity; if they can come at no evidence of the truth of Christianity, sufficient to induce 'em to sell all for Christ, in no other way than this.[17]

It remains before us then to determine how we shall come at the evidence of the truth of Christianity, for until now we have only the conflicting thesis that while there is available to the understanding only such knowledge of Christ as can be medi-

[15] *Works*, IV, 463.
[16] *Religious Affections*, ed. John Smith (New Haven, 1959), p. 303.
[17] *Ibid.*, p. 304.

ated through history a mere historical knowledge of Christ is not in itself sufficient to convince us of the truth.

The answer to this question has been clearly forecast in what we have seen previously of Edwards' thought. In one of the most precise statements of his position, he says that true saints apprehend Christ as he is presented by the gospel, but their apprehension has the character that they desire him above all other things for what he is in himself, for his "beauty," and for his "excellency." It is a sight, or a sense, of Christ's beauty and excellency

> that is the thing wherein does fundamentally consist the difference between those things in which the saving grace of God's Spirit consists, and the experience of devils and damned souls. This is the foundation of everything else that is distinguishing in true Christian experience.[18]

As we saw in the previous chapter the "beauty" of Christ consisted in the contrast which his purity and innocence struck with the ragged unevenness of evil in the world. What Edwards is adding to our metaphor of the canvas in the present discussion is that Christ truly becomes beautiful for us only when we see ourselves in the picture, only when we see that *we are the darkness for which Christ is the light*. In his own words, the saints will be moved by God's moral beauty only if they have "an answerable frame of heart, consisting in a disposition to abase themselves, and exalt God alone."[19] He who sustains such a view of himself while he "has his eyes open to behold the divine superlative beauty and loveliness of Jesus Christ," will not only be "convinced of Christ's sufficiency to stand as a mediator between him, a guilty, hell-deserving wretch, and an infinite holy God,"[20] but he will be overcome by an omnipotent

---

18 "A Divine and Supernatural Light," *Works*, IV, 469.
19 *Religious Affections*, p. 312.
20 "A Divine and Supernatural Light," *Works*, IV, 469.

power "so that now, not only the understanding but the will, and the whole soul, receives and embraces the Saviour."[21]

At the same time, Edwards is concerned to warn us against a potentially dangerous misinterpretation of this notion. He wants us to distinguish "between a willingness not to be damned, and a being willing to receive Christ for your Saviour."[22] Every man, even the devils, want to be saved from torment, but too often their desires are based on self-love. "Self-love is sufficient, without grace, to cause men to love those that love them, or that they imagine love them, and make much of them."[23] Edwards thinks it is quite possible to "love the deliverance, but hate the deliverer."[24] The reason men are naturally God's enemies is not that they prefer hell to God, but that they "see nothing in Christ wherefore they should desire him; no beauty or comeliness to draw or incline their hearts to him."[25] It is by the principle of self-love that some persons let their attention fall chiefly on their own experience.

> They keep thinking with themselves, what a good experience this is! What a great discovery this is! What wonderful things I have met with! And so they put their experience in the place of Christ, and his beauty and fullness.[26]

It is according to self-love that the viewer of Christ fails to see the entire canvas. He does not see that the brilliance of Christ is for the whole world; he sees only his own part in it, and thinks that Christ is solely for him. The entire work of God is then organized around the sinner and not around Christ.

Our understanding of the place of knowledge in faith will be further assisted if we observe the way in which Edwards

21 *Works,* IV, 470.
22 "Justice of God in the Damnation of Sinners," *Works,* IV, 241.
23 "A Divine and Supernatural Light," *Works,* IV, 467.
24 "Justice of God in the Damnation of Sinners," *Works,* IV, 242.
25 "Men Naturally God's Enemies," *Works,* IV, 57.
26 *Religious Affections,* p. 251.

uses his own favorite metaphor: light. Generally speaking, light for him is a synonym for knowledge, but knowledge in the double sense as a *penetration* of the mind, and as an *act* of the mind. In the first sense it is propositional knowledge, such as the knowledge of scripture, which enters the mind in the form of content, bringing light into the mind's darkness. In the second sense, it is a way of seeing; it is a kind of intentionality on the part of the viewer by which he is able to see beauty where others see only plainness. Light in the first sense is the usual sort of knowledge which we have already examined; it is according to the other kind of light that Edwards must carry his position. Now when we consider knowledge as an *act*, it is sharply to be distinguished from *information* or content. When Locke developed his theory of knowledge which led us to describe the mind as a container of skins from magic-onion substances, it was knowledge in the first, and not in the second, sense. As Edwards went beyond this as a boy, he does it again as a man.

There is a picturesque reference to the function of knowledge conceived as light in the second sense which he had written down in the *Miscellanies*—in one of those notes that cause the student of Edwards frequently to lament that he labored to keep his writing style so barren of poetic grace.

A man that sets himself to reason without divine light is like a man that goes in the dark into a garden full of the most beautiful plants, and most artfully ordered & compares things together by going from one thing to another to feel of them & to measure the distance: but he that sees by divine light is like a man that views the garden when the sun shines upon it. There is as it were a light cast upon the ideas of spiritual things in the mind of the believer which makes them appear clear & real which before were but faint obscure representations.[27]

27 *Miscellanies,* Yale MSS., No. 408.

Here we must observe that the man who "sees by divine light" sees nothing different from the other man. It is the same garden. The difference lies in the manner of perception. To the former man there is a clarity and reality to his perception that the other does not have.

Edwards has his attention focused here on an aspect of knowledge which he cannot find the adequate language or conceptual framework to describe. He makes the same point repeatedly and with little variation that when the soul is in receipt of spiritual light there is a much greater sense of the "reality" of divine things; indeed, of all things. True saints do not only have a predominating opinion that these things are true, "and so yield their assent, as they do in many other matters of doubtful speculation," he says in a curious locution, "but they see that it is really so: their eyes are opened, so that they see that really Jesus is the Christ, the Son of the living God."[28] Precisely what the difference is between seeing that Jesus is the Christ and seeing that he *really* is the Christ Edwards never succeeds in making clear. He is appealing simply to what he thinks will be our easily won credulity. It is true that in a loose sense most persons have the occasional experience of looking at something but not *really* seeing it. We read the words on a page, but we really are not reading them. We hear a funny tale, and we know that it is of the highest comedy, but we do not laugh. We see a person who has fallen into deep trouble, and we know the consequences will be dire if no one helps, but we pass on the other side.

This point has the appearance of a deep philosophical problem, but in fact it is rather from our own experience that we can provide some perspective for viewing this curious function of knowledge. Take, for example, the matter of reading printed words. It is altogether possible that we could be taught the pronunciation of a foreign language and even to read pages

[28] *Religious Affections,* p. 292.

of material without having the faintest notion of what it meant. Or we could read highly technical or poetic or allegorical language and have only a vague feeling that we were truly reading it. Usually we say that we have *really* read it when we have *understood* it. But what is understanding? Imagine coming across a document in which a revolutionary plan for the overthrow of the government is carefully detailed. We read it through, certain that we are able to understand what the author is concerned to say. Sometime later it befalls that we meet this author, and we tell him we have read his pamphlet. "Well, what did you do with it?" he asks immediately. We explain that we put it back on the shelf with the other revolutionary documents collected by our library. "But then you did not understand it," he exclaims sadly. "Otherwise you would have taken to the streets with cries of freedom and justice." Here the author has no interest in what may or may not have been in our minds in the form of knowledge content. He is concerned to see how the intentionality of our life has been altered by his words. We can be said really to have understood what he wrote only had there been a particular and visible alteration of our usual actions.

We shall not have violated the integrity of Edwards' thought if we say here that he has set before us a kind of knowing that finally has nothing to do with what happens "in our minds," but only in our visible lives. We *really know* what it means for a man to live in shame and indignity when we address our lives to the correction of the circumstances of his bondage. We *really know* what it means to have fallen among thieves when we dare to embrace the unnamed victim with our physical caring. We *really know* another person when we cross over the infinite distance that lies between our own comfortable and familiar circumstances and his strange and frightening circumstances.

We noted in the previous chapter that one of the aesthetic

principles by which Edwards executed his figurative portrait of Christ was that of contrast. Christ was pictured as the passive innocent in an age of brutally aggressive evil. He was the lamb who voluntarily gives himself to the compulsive savagery of fallen man. He was also the king who descends to take his place among the lowliest, who spares nothing in his devotion to even the worst of sinners. In the terms of the present chapter we can see that this is the picture of a Christ who *really understands* the world. This is a Christ who visibly crosses over to the circumstances of those who despise him the most. This is not the portrait of a man who is satisfied with a mere private piece of propositional knowledge about the corruption of the world, but of a man whose understanding of the world's failing causes him to overcome it with his own life.

In his definition of faith Edwards had us focus on scripture insofar as it exhibited Christ. Let us now say that scripture exhibits Christ when we can see him as the man who really knew the world, and when our so seeing him causes us also to know and understand the world in the same visible fashion. In other words, scripture becomes revelation when the beholder sees Christ as his most apparent good; when his will is as Christ is.

Lest the reader think we have run far beyond Edwards in these last reflections we must now pause to listen to him say some of this in language so awkward to the modern ear that we are likely, if not properly prepared for it, to disregard it. In more traditional language we are at that place in the theological structure where we are to talk about the union of the believer with Christ. This has not infrequently led to a sort of mysticism in the traditional discussion, and Edwards has himself been regarded as something of a mystic by some of his readers. When we remember that Christ for the saint is not a transcendent being somewhere removed from sense and sight, and capable of being perceived only through the transformation of the usual mental operations, but is rather the most apparent good, we can see how Edwards is capable of talking about a union with Christ that has nothing to do with a substantialist intermingling of two distinct beings. For he is saying simply that when he has true spiritual knowledge as we have been discussing it, *the saint is as the most apparent Christ is.*

> All the exercises of grace are entirely from Christ: but those exercises are not from Christ, as something that is alive, moves and stirs something that is without life, and yet remains without life; but as having life communicated to it; so as through Christ's power, to have inherent in itself, a vital nature. In the soul where Christ savingly is, there he lives. He don't actually live without it, so as violently to actuate it; but he lives in it; so that that also is alive.[29]

One of Edwards' favorite metaphors in this discussion is that of the arboreal graft. Into the *Images or Shadows of Divine Things* he had written a long entry dealing with this metaphor. According to one variation on this theme Christ is regarded as being grafted into the believer.

> All the fruit of the tree is by the ingrafting this tender twig into it. This ingrafted branch bears all. The tree in itself bears no good fruit, it is very sowr, but this ingrafted branch furnishes it. . . . The stock remains the same, but the fruit is altered. So, by Christ being ingrafted, the faculties of the soul are the same; there is the same human nature still, but there is a new fruit of grace, holy exercises and practice, and true blessedness.[30]

Here there is no mystical overflowing of the being of Christ into the being of the saint. When Christ lives "savingly" in

[29] *Religious Affections*, p. 342.
[30] *Images or Shadows of Divine Things*, ed. Perry Miller (New Haven, 1948), No. 166.

the soul, it means that the soul bears a new kind of fruit, a new way of living in the world. We saw above that Edwards could never concern himself, as the orthodox Reformed and Lutheran divines had, with the speculation as to the inner nature of Christ. He avoids the same sort of speculation here. Just as he was concerned with what *appears* in the life of Christ, so is his attention now on what *appears* in the life of the saint. Just as Christ could not exercise any influence on man except through what man could see in him, the saint cannot be said to be the recipient of divine grace unless that grace is visible to others.

VIII.

THE VISIBLE SAINT:
VIEWS FROM OLYMPUS
AND THE FIELD

It was in the year 1749 that Jonathan Edwards rose to take upon himself the mantle of prophet. The means by which he did so seem quaint and unimpressive to the modern sensibility. He published a short book, *An Humble Inquiry,* the sober and unembellished language of which struck a position that cut deeply across the almost universal inclinations of American society. Thanks partly to the gathering abundance of wealth and comfort, and thanks partly also to the humane accommodations to it on the part of his grandfather, it had become an implicit principle for most Americans of the age of Jonathan Edwards that religion was a private affair. The church's business in a world whose style of living is informed chiefly by the profit motive and the possession of property is to encourage the growth of personal piety. It is distinctly not the church's office to point to the discrepancies between the verbal expressions of a man's religious beliefs and the ethical conduct of his life. It is not the role of the religious man *really to understand* the world. With this "humble" book Edwards stood above his age not as a poet, not as a statesman, and not even as a preacher, but as a prophet who challenged his contemporaries to look at the world they had made, and to see that their journey was still unfinished.

The words of this book almost succeed in concealing from us the cyclonic reflection out of which they were written. Edwards coolly indicates in the preface that he could foresee the negative climate into which he was speaking.

> My appearing in this public manner on that side of the question, which is defended in the following sheets, will probably be surprising to many, as it is well known, that Mr. Stoddard, so great and eminent a divine, and my venerable predecessor in the pastoral office over the church in Northampton, as well as my own grandfather, publicly and strenuously appeared in opposition to the doctrine here maintained.[1]

The poignancy of this moment is magnified by the fact that Edwards' position on this question had very lately changed. He admits that he was formerly of the same opinion with his grandfather, "which I imbibed from his books, and have in my proceedings conformed to his practice; though never without some difficulties in my view, which I could not solve."[2] But two centuries later, the passions of the moment having vanished, the only surprising aspect of the position "defended in the following sheets," is that Edwards should have been so late in coming to it. As we have frequently observed, the heart of his thought from its very beginning required that the inward regeneration of the believer be attended with a corresponding visibility of it. And in the background of his own intellectual pilgrimage there lay a rich religious tradition in which this theme was prominent.

"The essence of Puritanism," Gordon Harland has written, "was always an intense experience of conversion that issued in

---

1 *Works* (see Chap. One, note 7), I, 85.
2 *Works*, I, 86.

a most disciplined effort to make the regenerate life visible and a profound conviction that God was using them to revolutionize human history."[3] In fact, Congregationalism, the ecclesiastical tradition in which Edwards ministered, carried the doctrine of visibility in its institutional memory. It was this principle "which gave significance to their demand for separation, in the first place."[4] It was thought that the church could covenant with itself, and could take upon itself the responsibility to judge its own orthodoxy in faith and practice through communal methods of self-examination. We find the principle plainly stated even in John Winthrop's sermon "On Boarde the Arrabella": "That which the most in theire Churches maineteine as a truthe in profession onely, wee must bring into familiar and constant practice."[5]

The "main question" of *An Humble Inquiry* is "whether according to the rules of Christ, any ought to be admitted to the communion and privileges of members of the visible church of Christ in complete standing, but such as are in profession, and in the eye of the church's Christian judgment, godly or gracious persons."[6] We are quickly given notice by Edwards that he will not be satisfied with a merely negative judgment that someone does not have signs of wickedness, but will look for a way of making the positive judgment that a person *does* have signs of true godliness.[7] Consistent with the thesis of his sermon on the experience of devils, he insists here that there "is no one qualification of mind whatsoever, that Christ has properly made the term of this [judgment]; not so much as a common belief that Jesus is the Messiah, or a belief

---

[3] "American Protestantism: Its Genius and Its Problem," *Drew Gateway,* XXXIV (Winter, 1964), 72.
[4] Geoffrey Nuttall, *Visible Saints, the Congregational Way 1640–1660* (Oxford, 1957), p. 131.
[5] Miller, Perry and Thomas H. Johnson, eds., *The Puritans* (New York, 1963), I, 198.
[6] *Works,* I, 89.   [7] *Works,* I, 95.

of the being of God. It is the credible profession and visibility
of these things, that is the church's rule in this case."[8]

Our attention is drawn to the word "credible" in this remark.
He is looking for some ground on which the manifestation of
true graciousness can be believed. He is looking for the kind
of "judgment wherein men do properly exercise reason, and
have their reason under the influences of love and other
Christian principles; which do not blind reason, but regulate
its exercises; being not contrary to reason, though they be very
contrary to censoriousness or unreasonable niceness and rigid-
ness."[9] Edwards does, of course, allow a distinction between
real and *visible* in one limited sense: God has given us no
certain rule by which the inner qualifications might be judged,
since these are out of the neighbor's view.[10] Visibility, therefore, "is a relative thing, and has relation to an eye that views
or beholds."[11] But, nonetheless, to say that a visible or apparent saint is *only* an apparent saint is nonsense. We shall
know none other than apparent saints.[12] The church is a gathering of persons who can know each other in no other way than as
they *appear* to each other. In his reading of history, and in his
familiarity with the Puritan story, not to mention his own experience during the Great Awakening, he had enough vivid examples of the danger that can be wrought if this notion be
abandoned, if it be thought that the judgment is to be made on
the basis of a reality which is not seen. He is only asking us to
see that by what appears in the communal life of the saints
there is adequate ground for a reasonable, credible judgment.

However, in the pages of the *Humble Inquiry* he does not
attempt to provide anything like a sufficient method for judging the evidence available in the apparent conduct of lives.
There are two other volumes in which this all-important task
is attempted, two very different volumes written at very dif-

[8] *Works*, I, 90.   [9] *Works*, I, 92.   [10] *Works*, I, 169.
[11] *Works*, I, 96.   [12] *Works*, I, 96f.

ferent periods of his life. Indeed, it is sometimes difficult to see how the same man could have written both of them. We shall first examine the essay on virtue which he had written toward the end of his ministry among the Indians. In the last year of his life he was invited to the presidency of Princeton College. In his letter of acceptance he confessed to what he thought would constitute a severe limitation on his ability to execute the duties of the office with the proper energy. "I have a constitution, in many respects peculiarly unhappy, attended with flaccid solids, vapid, sizy and scarce fluids, and a low tide of spirits; often occasioning a kind of childish weakness and contemptibleness of speech, presence, and demeanor, with a disagreeable dulness and stiffness, much unfitting me for conversation, but more especially for the government of a college."[13] As he composed this letter there lay on his desk a manuscript near completion. He called it a *Dissertation concerning the Nature of True Virtue,* and intended in its pages to set out a durable definition of this obscure subject. There is nothing vapid or sizy about this book. It is a fine, lean, beguilingly abstract statement.

"Whatever controversies and variety of opinions there are about the nature of virtue," he writes in the opening sentence, "yet all excepting some sceptics, who deny any real difference between virtue and vice, mean by it something beautiful, or rather some kind of beauty or excellency."[14] There are many kinds of beauty, of course, which are not properly regarded as virtue—such as the beauty of a building or a flower or of the harmony of the voice or even of the ideas of great statesmen and philosophers. But virtue is of a different kind of beauty; it is

13 *Jonathan Edwards, Representative Selections,* ed. Clarence Faust and Thomas Johnson (New York, 1962), p. 410.
14 *The Nature of True Virtue,* ed. William K. Frankena (Ann Arbor, Michigan, 1960), p. 1.

the beauty of those qualities and acts of the mind that are
of a moral nature, i.e., such as are attended with desert or
worthiness of praise or blame. Things of this sort it is generally agreed, so far as I know, do not belong merely to
speculation: but to the disposition and will, or (to use a
general word I suppose commonly well understood) to the
heart. Therefore I suppose I shall not depart from the common opinion when I say, that virtue is the beauty of the
qualities and exercises of the heart, or those actions which
proceed from them. So that when it is enquired, what is
the nature of true virtue? this is the same as to enquire what
that is, which renders any habit, disposition, or exercise of
the heart truly beautiful?[15]

Earlier we made reference to Edwards' distinction between
"general and particular beauty."[16] The latter has to do with
those exercises of the heart that issue from self-love and are
concerned with "some particular things within a limited, and as
it were a private sphere."

That only, therefore, is what I mean by true virtue, which,
belonging to the heart of an intelligent being, is beautiful
by a general beauty, or beautiful in a comprehensive view,
as it is in itself, and as related to every thing with which it
stands connected.[17]

With this remark he has prepared a clearing for the simple
but quite habitable definition of his subject:

True virtue most essentially consists in *benevolence to being
in general.* Or perhaps, to speak more accurately, it is that
consent, propensity and union of heart to being in general,
which is immediately exercised in a general good will.[18]

In the previous chapter we noted how spiritual knowledge
led to a style of living in the world, an act of will by which
the regenerate man becomes the light that shines into the

[15] *Ibid.*, pp. 1f.   [16] See above, pp. 75f.
[17] *The Nature of True Virtue,* p. 3.   [18] *Ibid.*

darkness of other lives. Now Edwards is giving abstract precision to that more impassioned view. By "being in general" Edwards does not mean the "idea of being," but rather *everything that is*. He is asking here that the man who dares to shape his life around the sort of love which Christ manifested in his life so relate himself to each aspect of this world, and each person in it, that it can be said he has taken the entire world into account and knows that this particular action is of greatest value to the whole. This is the man who refuses steadfastly to love only those who are of his party, and who are warmly engaged on his side, and promote his interest."[19] The man of true virtue would not take up military life merely out of a sense of deep affection for his nation, but only out of the conviction that his soldiering in this particular army and under these particular circumstances will prove to be of the greatest benevolence to the whole of mankind in the final accounting of history. The man of true virtue would not even espouse the business of his own church if he should see that this church has somehow fractured the beauty of its relationship with "being in general."

This definition of virtue fits in neatly with what we have so far seen in Edwards' life and thought, but there is nonetheless something spare and even barren about it; there is a cool rigidity running through these sentences. It has the character of being a final statement, a summary and conclusion to thoughts long in use. There is the sense that it has come from the hand of an old man whose mental powers are still clear and vigorous, but whose passions have yielded to reflection, frozen by the certain knowledge that the future held no more serious projects of the heart before him. We see no sign in these writings that when he has finished the page he will be eager to return to the Indian children; it seems rather that he would prefer to linger in the study and to let his mind feed

19 *Ibid.*, p. 47.

leisurely on the abstract elegance of its own operations. The wan intellectuality of this book easily misleads us; what Edwards is describing here in its broadest external outlines is the virtuous soul as it reproduces what he elsewhere calls the "excellency" or "beauty" of Christ. Christ's was the supreme consent of the soul to being in general.

A less olympian and schematic, but much more human, treatment of the regenerate will was written some fifteen years earlier. The *Treatise concerning the Religious Affections* was composed in the fading heat of the Awakening, as the wreckage of its excesses began to collect around him. Here he did not want to provide a grand design for the exercise of the will, but he wanted rather to provide some reliable way of determining "wherein those affections that are spiritual and gracious, do differ from those that are not so."[20] This was important to Edwards not simply because he needed analytical tools to deal with an immediate social problem, but because he had philosophical and theological convictions as to the centrality of the "affections" in human experience. The doctrine that stands behind this book is stated in the opening pages: "True religion, in great part, consists in holy affections."[21] Religiously considered, the doctrine was beyond dispute for Edwards. "That religion which God requires, and will accept," he concluded from his study of scripture, "does not consist in weak, dull and lifeless wouldings, raising us but a little above a state of indifference: God, in his Word, greatly insists upon it, that we be in good earnest, fervent in spirit, and our hearts vigorously engaged in religion."[22]

The word "affection" has fallen out of the usage common in Edwards' time. By his own definition "affections are no other, than the more vigorous and sensible exercises of the inclination and will of the soul."[23] Affections, then, are func-

[20] *Religious Affections,* ed. John Smith (New Haven, 1959), p. 193.
[21] *Ibid.,* p. 95.   [22] *Ibid.,* p. 99.   [23] *Ibid.,* p. 96.

tions of the will, but not apparently identical with the will itself. In giving this definition more precision Edwards adds, "The will, and the affections of the soul, are not two faculties; the affections are not essentially distinct from the will, nor do they differ from the mere actings of the will and inclination of the soul, but only in the liveliness and sensibleness of exercise."[24] If the affections are livelier than the "mere actings of the will," they are also less violent than the passions.

> The *affections* and *passions* are frequently spoken of as the same; and yet, in the more common use of speech, there is in some respect a difference; and affection is a word, that in its ordinary signification, seems to be something more extensive than passion; being used for all vigorous lively actings of the will or inclination; but passion for those that are more sudden, and whose effects on the animal spirits are more violent, and the mind more overpowered, and less in its own command.[25]

Edwards' use of the term "affection" is also to be distinguished from the current use of "experience" and "emotion." Both of these latter words apply to more passive states of human agency and intellection, although Edwards is at some pains to indicate that in true affection there is a considerable amount of what we generally refer to as subjective or personal feeling. In either case, it is striking that when he comes to judge the authenticity of the affections he does so according to certain visible *signs*. Again we are reminded that Edwards will not allow us to keep our beetles hidden; the interiority of religious experience is not to be separated from the exteriority of ethical action.

He begins this long examination by listing "some things, which are no signs that affections are gracious, or that they are not." These are what might be called neutral signs. " 'Tis no sign one way or the other," for example, "that religious af-

[24] *Ibid.*, p. 97.   [25] *Ibid.*, p. 98.

fections are very great, or raised very high."[26] True affections should be high because their object is a very great being, but still there is evidence in scripture and in experience that "there are religious affections which are very high, that are not spiritual and saving."[27] Nor 'tis it a "sign that affections have the nature of religion, or that they have not, that they have great effects on the body."[28] Anyone can "see that such effects oftentimes arise from great affections about temporal things, and when religion is no way concerned in them."[29] Those who are "fluent, fervent and abundant, in talking of the things of religion," are for that reason alone not to be judged as to the true graciousness of their affections.[30] Even if one cannot put his finger on the natural cause of his affections there is no reason to think that they therefore originate in a supernatural grace.[31] For " 'tis God's manner," Edwards says in a telling sentence,

> in the great works of his power and mercy which he works for his people, to order things so, as to make his hand visible, and his power conspicuous, and men's dependence on him most evident, that no flesh should glory in his presence. . . . and none might say mine own hand hath saved me.[32]

It is clearly not enough to know that it is not by my hand; there must be some visible evidence that it was by God's hand. But we shall not learn whether those visible actions are of God simply because the affections they express "come with texts of scripture, remarkably brought to the mind."[33] Nor even if there "is an appearance of love in them."[34] There are many kinds of love which prove under trial to be counterfeit. Even if we find that a person has affections of many kinds

[26] *Ibid.*, p. 127. [27] *Ibid.*, p. 130. [28] *Ibid.*, p. 131.
[29] *Ibid.*, p. 132. [30] *Ibid.*, p. 135. [31] *Ibid.*, p. 138.
[32] *Ibid.*, p. 139f. [33] *Ibid.*, p. 142. [34] *Ibid.*, p. 146.

exhibiting a certain symmetry, there is no good reason to think they are gracious.[35]

> The various faculties, principles and affections of the human nature, are as it were many channels from one fountain: if there be sweet water in the fountain, sweet water will from thence flow out into those various channels; but if the water in the fountain be poisonous, then poisonous streams will also flow out into all those channels. So that the channels and streams will be alike, corresponding one with another; but the great difference will lie in the nature of the water.[36]

If the nature of the water is not disclosed by the variety of fountains one may just as well say that nothing can "be determined concerning the nature of the affections by this, that comforts and joys seem to follow awakenings and convictions of conscience, in a *certain order*."[37] This last may be one of the most interesting of the neutral signs since it was common at the time to judge the verity of an affection by whether it followed a legal conviction of sin. No one knew better than Edwards that even if persons have had "great terrors, which really have been from the awakening and convincing influences of the Spirit of God," it is still possible that the "unmortified corruption of the heart may quench the Spirit of God (after he has been striving) by leading men to presumptuous, and self-exalting hopes and joys, as well as otherwise."[38] And if we wonder whether there be sufficient self-mortification to render those legal frightenings fruitful, we shall not be able to judge by observing that persons are "zealously engaged in the external duties of worship."[39] And no more reliable will our knowledge be if we see mouths opening to praise and glorify God,[40] or if persons are "exceeding confident that what they

---

[35] *Ibid.,* p. 147. [36] *Ibid.,* p. 151. [37] *Ibid.*
[38] *Ibid.,* p. 157. [39] *Ibid.,* p. 163. [40] *Ibid.,* p. 165.

experience is divine, and that they are in a good estate."[41] Some will make strong outward manifestations of true affection designed to please those who are truly godly,[42] but such manifestations are no basis of judgment, just as the nature of a tree cannot be determined apart from the fruit which it will bear.[43]

These neutral signs are as much the reflections of the pastor as they are the analysis of the philosopher, for both knew that unless that which appears in the behavior of the saints be grounded in something more enduring than the mere pleasure which the affections provide, those affections would vanish. They both knew that private intercourse between the creature and his creator caused one to withdraw from meaningful talk and action in the world; but at the same time they knew that the saint's life in the world had to be of a quality radically different from that of the natural man, and not merely in the *design* of it, but especially in the *fruit* of it.

Thus when he comes to the "positive" signs he calls first upon those themes which inform his theology from its very center, and which run just under the surface of every section of his thought. First, true affections "do arise from those influences and operations on the heart, which are *spiritual, supernatural* and *divine.*"[44] But this won't be known by looking on that metaphorical point where the supernatural light strikes the soul, but rather by seeing whether there is evidenced in his life the "new simple idea" of Christ—whether, in other words, Christ is the *reason* for his acting as he does. In the second sign, which Edwards calls the "first objective ground of gracious affections," he underlines the importance that it be *Christ* who is our reason and not some pleasantness of emotion within ourselves.[45] In the third sign, Edwards reminds us that the excellency of divine things is primarily a *moral* excellency; it

41 *Ibid.*, p. 167. 42 *Ibid.*, p. 181. 43 *Ibid.*, p. 185.
44 *Ibid.*, p. 197. 45 *Ibid.*, pp. 240ff.

must result not in contemplation but in action. Christ is not equivalent to reason, but is rather equivalent to the *reason for our actual behavior*. But in the fourth sign, he cautions us against assuming that the heart is involved in the affair at the expense of the mind: "Gracious affections do arise from the mind's being enlightened, rightly and spiritually to understand or apprehend divine things."[46] Christ will become our reason only through the manner of his appearance, though he will not be our greatest apparent good until we have "a certain kind of ideas or sensations of mind, which are simply diverse from all that is or can be in the minds of natural men."[47] And yet this diversity does not mean that we are therefore sundered from the regulation of reason for, as he puts it in the fifth sign, "truly gracious affections are attended with a reasonable and spiritual conviction of the judgment, of the reality and certainty of divine things."[48] Affections are never entirely distinct from beliefs, from the intellectual assent to the propositions of divinity—although for Edwards this is always an assent "founded on real evidence, or upon that which is a good reason, or just ground of conviction."[49]

And if we wonder precisely where that spiritual exercise of reason departs from the natural use of it, Edwards tells us in the sixth sign that there is a legal repentance, or conviction of our sinfulness, that can come by means of the merely sequential cogitation of any man. The man who reasons according to a spiritual and gracious sense is convinced "of his own utter insufficiency, despicableness, and odiousness," and joined to that conviction is "an answerable frame of heart."[50] The spiritual exercise of reason is visible only when it is evident that one has based his behavior in the world on nothing that will work to his own gain, but rather looks outward with an obvious passion of self-denial.

[46] *Ibid.*, p. 266.   [47] *Ibid.*, p. 271.   [48] *Ibid.*, p. 291.
[49] *Ibid.*, p. 295.   [50] *Ibid.*, p. 311.

But such self-denial is no ephemeral characteristic of the saints, Edwards tells us in the seventh sign, for one of the ways in which "gracious affections are distinguished from others, is, that they are attended with a change of nature."[51] If we take the term "nature" not to refer to the substantive, physical presence of the person, but to what he *habitually does* by nature,[52] then we learn from this observation that the affections which evidence a reasonable self-denial are authentic only when one persists in such self-denial, only when it has become further obvious that such self-denial as can be seen in him in the present is not merely for a greater self-gratification in the end. But self-denial, whether it be reasonable or no, is negative. Edwards does not intend this to be an action in itself, but rather to make room for what is the truly gracious action of the soul. And when we ask what that truly gracious action is, we remember that what is made visible in us is not simply our own actions, but by virtue of Christ, we make him visible as well. Therefore, in the eighth sign, he tells us that

> truly gracious affections differ from those affections that are false and delusive, in what they tend to, and are attended with the lamblike, dovelike spirit and temper of Jesus Christ; or, in other words, they naturally beget and promote such a spirit of love, meekness, quietness, forgiveness and mercy, as appeared in Christ.[53]

How prominent the theme of the union of the saint with Christ is in Edwards appears here where instead of developing a picture of the *exemplary* relation between Christ and the believer, he explains that it

> would be strange if Christians should not be of the same temper and spirit that Christ is of; when they are his flesh

[51] *Ibid.*, p. 340.
[52] Cf. the discussion of the way in which man's sinfulness, in Edwards' conception of it, is made synonymous with man's nature, Chapter Four, above.
[53] *Religious Affections*, p. 345.

> and his bone, yea are one spirit (I Cor. 6:17), and live so, that it is not they that live, but Christ that lives in them. A Christian spirit is Christ's mark, that he sets upon the souls of his people; his seal is in their foreheads, bearing his image and superscription.[54]

Hardly distinguishable from the eighth sign is the ninth: "Gracious affections soften the heart, and are attended and followed with a Christian tenderness of spirit."[55]

When one looks over all of these signs and characteristics of true gracious affections, he will find that one of the ways in which they may be distinguished from false affections is their beautiful symmetry and proportion.

> In the truly holy affections of the saints is found that proportion which is the natural consequence of the universality of their sanctification. They have the whole image of Christ upon them: they have "put off the old man, and have put on the new man" entire in all his parts and members.[56]

Here Edwards is looking at the basic integrity of the exercise of true affections; there must be something about them that is convincing with regard to the continuity and consistency there is throughout the whole of a person's actions. And, moreover, there must appear in them, to be convincing, a spontaneity and an eagerness to continue in spiritual exercise. Gracious affections do not rest satisfied in themselves; on the contrary, "the higher they are raised, the more is a spiritual appetite and longing of soul after spiritual attainments, increased."[57]

Above these eleven signs is erected still another: that perduring insistence of Edwards' that every influence of the spirit must issue in "holy practice." The twelfth sign is not so much an addition to those preceding it as it is a summary of

[54] *Ibid.*, p. 347.   [55] *Ibid.*, p. 357.   [56] *Ibid.*, p. 365.
[57] *Ibid.*, p. 376.

all the others. It is that necessary condition without which it is meaningless to discuss the other signs. For to say that "gracious and holy affections have their exercise and fruit in Christian practice," is to imply three things of the believer:

(1) That his behavior or practice in the world, be universally conformed to, and directed by Christian rules. (2) That he makes a business of such a holy practice above all things; that it be a business which he is chiefly engaged in, and devoted to, and pursues with highest earnestness and diligence: so that he may be said to make this practice of religion eminently his work and business. And (3) That he persists in it to the end of his life.[58]

This book combines the keen, empirical eye of the preacher who has spent the bulk of his mature years looking into the lives of his people to discern where and how his ministry is bearing fruit, with the agile, contemplative mind restlessly in search of greater clarity through distinction. The maturity and the carefulness, the almost total absence of rancor, that characterize this volume make it difficult to deny that there could be a perspective from which the authenticity of the Christian life could be *reasonably* judged. Edwards does not once fall into cavilling narrowness or sheer, groundless assertion in this volume, nor is there once an absence of human sensitivity in the statement of his acute definitions and observations. It is a compassionate work by a reasonable man. When we consider that it was written at a moment of great spiritual confusion in the life of Northampton it is all the more striking.

Once the olympian perspective of the dissertation into the nature of true virtue has been combined with the battlefield wisdom of the treatise concerning the religious affections, to provide us with the specific principles by which the visibility of grace is to be adjudged, we are faced with the question as to who will make the judgment. On this question Edwards

[58] *Ibid.,* p. 383.

has not the slightest hesitation: it is the church in whom this prerogative rests.

> I say in the eye of the church's Christian judgment, because it is properly a visibility to the eye of the public charity, and not of a private judgment, that gives a person the right to be received as a visible saint by the public.[59]

It is primarily the private judgment of the minister which Edwards is concerned to eliminate by this distinction, because the minister, in receiving one "to the communion of the church, is to act as a public officer, and in behalf of the public society, and not merely for himself, and therefore is to be governed in acting, by a proper visibility of godliness in the eye of the public."[60]

This judgment is relinquished to the church because, for one thing, it is more likely to be accurate when made communally. The probability of accuracy, Edwards speculated, was about ten to one.[61] For another, the very nature of the church makes it both necessary and fitting. "Another evidence," Edwards says, "that such as are taken into the church, ought to be in the eye of a Christian truly *gracious* or *pious* persons, is this, that the Scripture represents the *visible church* of Christ as a society having its several members united by the bond of *Christian brotherly love.*"[62] There is a distinguishing kind of affection saints have for one another—a oneness of heart, a *philadelphia.*[63] It is impossible that there exist such an affection toward brethren in Christ unless there be a sound apprehension or judgment of the mind as to the foundation of that affection.

> To say, that we must thus *love* others as visible members of Christ, if anything *else* be meant than that we must love them because they are visibly, or *as* they appear to our judg-

[59] "A Humble Inquiry," *Works,* I, 92.
[60] *Works,* I, 92. [61] *Works,* I, 93. [62] *Works,* I, 142.
[63] *Works,* I, 142.

ment, real members of Christ, is in effect to say, that we must thus love them without any foundation at all.[64]

There is one final feature of Edwards' position on this question which we could overlook only by way of giving considerable distortion to the entire discussion. From the beginning he has assumed that visibility is attended with *oral profession.* On the face of it, oral profession would seem unnecessary, especially in light of the clear principles by which visible actions can be judged. We would certainly not judge a man saved simply because he said he was; nor would we consider him without grace if he said nothing. And yet, it is necessary to Edwards' view that profession and visibility are kept bound together, for once they are sundered the language of faith loses its meaning. A man might talk eloquently about his own soul and his taste for things of the spirit, but this in itself is not enough.

> Thus, for instance, if a man, using an equivocal term, should say, that such an evening a king was in that room, without any marks of difference or discrimination whatsoever, by which others could discern whether by a king, he meant the ruler of a kingdom, or a king used in a game of chess: the word thus used would be no declaration that the head of a kingdom was there at such a time; nor would they give any notice of any such thing to those to whom he spoke, or give them any rational ground to understand or judge any such thing.[65]

If there are no reliable rules governing the connections between the way words are used and the actions of the persons who uses them, then the words mean nothing in particular. In fact, they can be used in any situation. Edwards knew that when this happened all of the talk about America's future, or the "benevolent smiles of providence" upon her history, would

---

[64] *Works,* I, 144.   [65] *Works,* I, 220.

be mere pious cant. Men could then use the great sentences of the Bible to give added, but deceptive, luster to whatever it is they are doing at the time. Edwards knew that once oral profession of faith and the visibility of it were separated the voice of the prophet would go unheard in the cacophonous verbal confusion of the world.

This is a point of considerable importance in the present age. It is the experience of modern man that he is awash in a plethora of words that only faintly betoken an identifiable set of actions. Men call on the name of God to guarantee the greater murderousness of their warring; and by the name of the same God do others cry for peace. By a profession of biblical faith some build angry walls of racial and economic separation between themselves and others; by the same faith some turn back not even from death in the cause of social justice; and still others curl protectively around their private ecstasies in the suave quiet of carpeted churches, blind both to hatred and to the energies bravely spent overcoming hatred.

But the bottomless chaos of shifting meanings has claimed much more than the idioms of religious discourse. Presidents and premiers, ministers and senators pronounce over their national policies fine rhetorical sentences about universal peace and a fruitful brotherliness, but those policies seem never to diminish the hegemony of darkness in the affairs of men. Universities summon inquiring minds to an unrestricted freedom in the pursuit of truth, but attempt to guarantee the defenders of current moral convention and political strategy that the truth will not prove an offense to those who did not bother to pursue it. There has appeared a blurring vagueness in the line that once distinguished profanity from propriety, and blasphemy from personal integrity.

Northampton was a town of a few thousand souls, but what happened in Northampton has happened in a nation of a few hundred million souls. And what was heard in Northampton in the year 1749 brought the same vigorous rejection that an America two centuries older would still bring to the same words. When Edwards asked for the integrity of profession he was asking that when men fill their mouths with words of peace and truth and affection, they may also be expected to fill their lives with the earnest pursuit of these things.

But when he asked that visibility be joined to a *profession of Christian faith* he was asking for something still more radically revolutionary. For by this conception of faith and its relation to the world Edwards was asking that the church be a community of men who clearly understand their office in the world to be the vanguard, the first legion, in the long journey toward the ultimate society. They must not only be ahead of the world in this journey, but they must make so visible in their present life together the nature of that ultimate society that the world would eagerly follow them. Edwards was now standing where Winthrop had stood. Over the horizon there lay the promised fortunes of God's unrestrained bounty. Before him was not only a congregation, but a civilization. The church, Edwards was saying in the supreme moment of his life, must become the most apparent good for the world.

When the church came to make their decision, they spoke not only for the first American century that lay behind them, they spoke also for the two American centuries yet to come. Twenty-three cast their votes for Jonathan Edwards; two hundred and thirty voted to relieve him of his pastoral office. Ten to one.

IX.

AN URGENT *NOW!* FOR
THE LANGUID WILL

*T*he alert reader will have become increasingly aware that the course of the portraiture to this point has made at least one rather obvious circumvention. Perhaps there is the suspicion that something is being intentionally omitted, and like the official portraits of Lenin after the revolution the "message" has overwhelmed and obscured the "facts" of the original event. What every living man could have remembered about Lenin and the revolution was that it was a season of uncommon anguish in which the innocent perished in number as generous as the confusion of the age was great. Where does that appear on the epic canvas? Or like the artist whose executed work is designed merely to flatter its subject, we might be accused of having left out the withered leg. Not just once, but with surprising frequency, Jonathan Edwards delivered the most searing maledictions in the memory of the American church.

What must be said at once is that there is no way of avoiding this fact. We cannot say, for example, that Edwards was momentarily taken up into the reckless spirit of the Awakening, or that he did not "really believe" what he was saying. The eternal torment of the damned was a subject to which he repeatedly and tirelessly turned in his preaching, and even in his miscellaneous notes. There is no item in this vivid explosion of metaphoric carnage on which his imagination could not feed at length. Indeed, we might well argue that his creative powers are nowhere more in evidence than in these astonishing pages. Our task in interpreting this material is the same as it has been elsewhere: we must not merely record our reactions to it, but attempt to understand what it *meant* for Edwards to believe that there was a hell and that its purpose was to punish sinners.

In agreement with virtually every other major thinker in the Western world before him, Edwards uncritically accepted the theory of immortality. Without argument or defense he could plainly say that "intelligent beings of the world are everlasting & will remain after the world comes to an end."[1] But what gives specific shape to his thinking about the after-world comes from another more or less implicit theme, also widely shared, that the inner logic of the ethical life could be comprehended in the term "desert." A man gets what he deserves. The patient seeker after truth, the doer of righteousness, the faithful servant, each shall be rewarded for his uprightness and earnestness. But, since the world in which we live is a world largely without Edwards' "beauty" and "excellency" no such perfect recompense in the mortal life can be expected. For in this life the innocent will suffer and the wicked prosper. Therefore, final rewards and debts will be paid and collected in the world to come. Immanuel Kant was so persuaded of the idea of just deserts that he thought the ethical life made belief in immortality necessary.[2]

Consistent with these two themes there is an overall design to the imprecatory sermons that the casual reader, interested

---

[1] *Miscellanies*, Yale MSS., No. 547.
[2] Cf. *Critique of Pure Reason*, trans. Lewis White Beck (Indianapolis, 1956), pp. 126ff.

more in amusement than in understanding, will easily overlook.
First, we should observe the way in which the torments of hell
have been described. With what must have been great effectiveness Edwards reaches into the common experience of his
listeners to convey their imagination by means of vivid sense
impression into the eternal anguish. Appealing to the universal
dread of being locked into a closed place without any hope
of escape, for instance, he says that hell "is a strong prison:
it is beyond any finite power, or the united strength of all
wicked men and devils to unlock, or break open the door of
that prison. Christ hath the key of hell; 'he shuts and no man
opens.' "[3] There were few experiences in the frontier town
that were more terrifying than housefires: "Some of you have
seen buildings on fire; imagine therefore with yourselves, what
a poor hand you would make at fighting with the flames, if
you were in the midst of so great and fierce a fire."[4] In the
same sermon he introduces the famous image of the spider in
the flames, combining it with the common miniature drama
of the moth or mayfly led by its own fascination into the
candle flame.

> You have often seen a spider, or some other noisome insect,
> when thrown into the midst of a fierce fire, and have ob-
> served how immediately it yields to the force of the flames.
> There is no long struggle, no fighting against the fire, no
> strength exerted to oppose the heat, or to fly from it; but it
> immediately stretches forth itself and yields; and the fire
> takes possession of it, and at once it becomes full of fire,
> and is burned into a bright coal.[5]

Once he has the wicked in the midst of the fierce heat, defenseless against it, he will not let them find any place of
refuge, "any secret corner, which will be cooler than the rest,

---

[3] "The Future Punishment of the Wicked Unavoidable and Intolerable,"
Works, (see Chap. One, note 7), IV, 259.
[4] *Works*, IV, 263f.   [5] *Works*, IV, 264.

where they may have a little respite, a small abatement of the extremity of their torment. They never will be able to find any cooling stream or fountain, in any part of that world of torment; no nor so much as a drop of water to cool their tongues." Edwards wants his auditors to see that once the wrath of God has been unleashed on a sinner, he can avoid it no more easily than a worm can lift the heavy rock thrown down upon it.[6]

In perhaps the most severe of all his sermons Edwards reaches much closer to the heart. He concludes from his studies of scripture that when the last judgment has been made and when the whole of mankind has been divided into the saved and the damned, "the two worlds of happiness and misery will be in view of each other." "The saints in glory will see how the damned are tormented: they will see God's threatenings fulfilled, and his wrath executed upon them."[7] This gives him the chance to say that since this division will be by God's justice, and since every saint loves God's justice, there "will be none to pity you."

> Look which way you will, before or behind, on the right hand or left, look up to heaven, or look about you in hell, and you will see none to condole your case, or to exercise any pity towards you, in your dreadful condition. You must bear these flames, you must bear that torment and amazement, day and night, forever, and never have the comfort of considering, that there is so much as one that pities your case; there never will one tear be dropped for you.[8]

The emotional climax of this sermon is a passage that bids fair to be cited as the moment of greatest power—or perhaps savagery—in the entire genre. He asks the unregenerate within

[6] *Works,* IV, 259.
[7] "The End of the Wicked Contemplated by the Righeous: or the Torments of the Wicked in Hell, No Occasion of Grief to the Saints in Heaven," *Works,* IV, 289.
[8] *Works,* IV, 294f.

his hearing to think of their friends, and especially their parents, when the final judgment is uttered.

How will you bear to see your parents, who in this life had so dear an affection for you, now without any love to you, approving the sentence of condemnation, when Christ shall with indignation bid you depart, wretched, cursed creatures, into eternal burnings? How will you bear to see and hear them praising the Judge, for his justice exercised in pronouncing this sentence, and hearing it with holy joy in their countenances, and shouting forth the praises and hallelujahs of God and Christ on that account? When they shall see what manifestations of amazement there will be in you, at the hearing of this dreadful sentence, and that every syllable of it pierces you like a thunderbolt, and sinks you into the lowest depths of horror and despair; when they shall behold you with a frightened, amazed countenance, trembling and astonished, and shall hear you groan and gnash your teeth; these things will not move them at all to pity you, but you will see them with a holy joyfulness in their countenances, and with songs in their mouths. When they shall see you turned away and beginning to enter into the great furnace, and shall see how you shrink at it, and hear how you shriek and cry out; yet they will not be at all grieved for you, but at the same time you will hear from them renewed praises and hallelujahs for the true and righteous judgments of God, in so dealing with you.[9]

If these are the words of man become captive to an extreme religious position, they are also the words of an artist, for Edwards, with a skill as sure as that of any story teller, has collapsed the distance between his subject matter and his listeners by describing a strange and terrifying world in terms of a present and familiar world. But there is a decisive difference between what Edwards is doing here and what a teller of stories seeks to accomplish. A story is designed to arrest the

[9] *Works,* IV, 296.

fancy, freeing it from the immediate world, in order that momentarily the listener will be suspended from the present-ness of his experience. Edwards' appeal is not to the fancy, but to the will. He is not giving us a world that will exist if only we can take our attention from the immediately given; he is giving us a world in which we will exist if we fail to heed the true nature of the immediately given. Edwards is giving us a world which our present wills surely will create if they persist in the spiritual languor. Look where you are now, he is saying. Not then, but NOW!

If any of the saints will need assistance in determining how their will is faring, Mr. Edwards can provide that, too, in these sermons. "Look over your past life," he calls out to them, "inquire at the mouth of conscience, and hear what that has to testify concerning it."[10] Then like a surgeon in search of the body's disease, he pokes into the private reflections of his listeners, attempting to startle them into an awareness of their peccability.

> How many sorts of wickedness have you been guilty of!

> How manifold have been the abominations of your life! What profaneness and contempt of God has been exercised by you!

> And how have you behaved yourself in the time of family prayer!

> What wicked carriage have some of you been guilty of toward your parents! How far have you been from paying that honor to them that God has required!

> How have some of you vaunted yourselves in your apparel! Others in their riches! Others in their knowledge and abilities! How has it galled you to see others above you!

10 "The Justice of God in the Damnation of Sinners," *Works,* IV, 232.

And what abominable lasciviousness have some of you been guilty of! How have you indulged yourself from day to day, and from night to night, in all manner of unclean imaginations! Has not your soul been filled with them, till it has become a hold of foul spirits, and a cage of every unclean and hateful bird?[11]

After this catalogue of personal failings comes the concluding, summarizing question: "Now, can you think when you have thus behaved yourself, that God is obliged to show you mercy? Are you not, after all this, ashamed to talk of its being hard with God to cast you off?"[12]

The most famous of all Edwards' sermons, "Sinners in the Hands of an Angry God," is not properly a description of hell as such. It is concerned rather with the fact that the time between the present and one's death is a totally unknown quantity. Death comes suddenly and unannounced.

The unseen, unthought of ways and means of persons' going suddenly out of the world are innumerable and inconceivable. Unconverted men walk over the pit of hell on a rotten covering, and there are innumerable places in this covering so weak that they will not bear their weight, and these places are not seen. The arrows of death fly unseen at noonday; the sharpest sight cannot discern them.[13]

The imagery of the sermon is designed to communicate the sense of a disaster close at hand.

There are the black clouds of God's wrath now hanging directly over your heads, full of the dreadful storm, and big with thunder; and were it not for the restraining hand of God, it would immediately burst forth upon you. The sovereign pleasure of God, for the present, stays his rough wind: otherwise it would come with fury, and your destruc-

11 *Works,* IV, 233f.   12 *Works,* IV, 235.
13 *Works,* IV, 315.

tion would come like a whirlwind, and you would be like
the chaff of the summer threshing floor.[14]

In the conclusion to the sermon the imagery falls away and
the minister confronts his congregation with direct prose
plainly describing their situation.

> There is reason to think that there are many in this con-
> gregation now hearing this discourse, that will actually be
> the subjects of this very misery to all eternity. We know
> not who they are, or in what seats they sit, or what thoughts
> they now have. It may be they are now at ease, and hear
> all these things without much disturbance, and are now
> flattering themselves that they are not the persons; promising
> themselves that they shall escape. . . . But alas! . . . how
> many is it likely will remember this discourse in hell! And
> it would be a wonder, if some that are now present would
> not be in hell in a very short time, before this year is out.
> And it would be no wonder if some persons, that now sit
> here in some seats of this meeting-house in health, and
> quiet and secure, should be there before to-morrow morn-
> ing.[15]

The purpose of such preaching is certainly clear enough. It
can be summarized in one straightforward sentence of Edwards': "The only opportunity of escaping is in this world;
this is the only state of trial wherein we have any offers of
mercy, or there is any place for repentance."[16] To draw a heavy
line of emphasis under this fact, he wants to make it understood by all that with death each person has lost the last
chance to change the final balance of his life. After death
there are no more chances, there is no hope whatsoever, for
the torments of hell are eternal.

> How dismal will it be, when you are under these racking
> torments, to know assuredly that you never, never shall be

14 *Works,* IV, 317.   15 *Works,* IV, 321.
16 "The Eternity of Hell Torments," *Works,* IV, 275f.

delivered from them; to have no hope: when you shall wish that you might but be turned into nothing, but shall have no hope of it; when you shall wish that you might be turned into a toad or a serpent, but shall have no hope of it; when you would rejoice, if you might but have any relief, after you shall have endured these torments millions of ages, but shall have no hope of it; when after you shall have worn out the age of the sun, moon, and stars, in your dolorous groans and lamentations, without any rest day or night, or one minute's ease, yet you shall have no hope of ever being delivered.[17]

The undeniable contempt the preacher is pouring out in these words serves easily to obscure another rather remarkable feature of Edwards' imprecatory sermons. While he is convinced of man's mountainous sinfulness, he is also saying that a man's entire life, both past and future, lies under the power of his present will. All of a man's debts for things past, and all of a man's responsibilities for things to come, are fully within the power of his present will to discharge. What lies behind these sermons, therefore, is Edwards' profound respect for both the importance and power of the human will. This point is made all the clearer when we see how he deals with the opposite side of this same subject matter; that is, when he addresses himself to the consequences that attend the life of a man who had seized on Christ as his most apparent good. Such a man, in Edwards' judgment, was David Brainerd.

In 1747 young Brainerd, missionary to the Indians and fiance of Edwards' daughter, Jerusha, died of tuberculosis in the Edwards home. A few months later Jerusha, carrying Brainerd's love and his disease, followed him to the grave. Brainerd had asked Edwards on his deathbed to edit his private journals. *The Life and Diary of David Brainerd* fell into the long tradition of Puritan pieces in which the diarist painfully ex-

17 *Works*, IV, 278.

amines himself against standards for his performance that could not possibly be met. It reads therefore like a mournful self-condemnation, but in the idiom of the time it could be seen as the modestly composed chronicle of a spiritual hero willing to undergo any danger and hardship in the service of his Lord. Brainerd's funeral sermon was preached by Edwards, and is memorable if only because the preacher converts his transparent grief into a long discourse on the experience of the saints after death. Like the damned in hell, the saints' blessedness in heaven is eternal. And as the damned are thrown into the keeping of Satan, the saints are led into the presence of Christ.

> The most intimate intercourse becomes that relation that the saints stand in to Jesus Christ; and especially becomes that most perfect and glorious union they shall be brought into with him in heaven. They are not merely Christ's servants, but his friends.[18]

The experience of the saint in life is, as we have seen, one of great affection. When Christ becomes one's most apparent good, he responds with love for all things. In heaven the appearance of Christ will be more direct, and the response to it all the more vivid, for there the elect

> see every thing in Christ that tends to kindle and inflame love, and every thing that tends to gratify love, and every thing that tends to satisfy them: and that in the most clear and glorious manner, without any darkness or delusion, without any impediment or interruption.[19]

Edwards described the life of the saint on earth as one of vital union with Christ. After death this union becomes much more complete. The saints not only live by his life, but they also share in his power and glory; they are

[18] "Saints When Absent from the Body," *Works*, III, 629.
[19] *Works*, III, 627f.

exalted to reign with him. They are through him made kings and priests, and reign with him, and in him, over the same kingdom. As the Father hath appointed unto him a kingdom, so he has appointed the Son to reign over his kingdom, and the Son appoints his saints to reign in his.[20]

Here again we can focus on the mythic absurdity of these thoughts, or we can attempt to get behind them and to understand why Edwards should have voiced them in this way and on this occasion. If it is the case that the sermons on hell are designed to awaken the people into a recognition of the power of the will, then so is this sermon and the others like it. If they can choose hell, they can also choose heaven. The vast differences between heaven and hell point to the vast differences between the kinds of lives people currently are living. The one is dark and self-enclosed, turned in upon itself, feeding on its own emotions and organizing all values around its own needs and tastes. The other is brilliantly life-affirming, it is open and free, seeing in the darkness not the estuary of its self-destruction but the possibility of new and surprising kinds of caring for the world. Jonathan Edwards thought that Brainerd had lived the latter kind of life, and this sermon is a way of saying it. "Saints When Absent from the Body," is not a disembodied, ill-informed series of speculations about some other world; it is a profound HURRAH! for the life of David Brainerd.

Therefore, I shall make no attempt here to omit from this portrait what many have regarded as the least creditable part of Jonathan Edwards' intellectual production. On the contrary, the portrait would lose much of its power and meaning if the blacker machinations of this American intelligence were left out of it. For in these sermons are combined what Americans elsewhere are wont to celebrate in the worldliness of their civilization: a hard-minded appraisal of the nature of things

20 *Works,* III, 631.

as they are, and a sturdy confidence that by an act of the will all things are alterable.

Edwards looked out upon his world and what he saw there was not beautiful. We are momentarily deceived by the fact that what he thought was ugliness is for us a series of petty moral failings, because the ugliness of our own age stands in such contrast to his. He was worried about children being distracted from family prayer; but we have seen the family structure itself fall into decay. He was alarmed by those who vaunted themselves in their apparel and in their riches; but we live in an age when a man's wealth brings upon him an astonishing blindness to the poverty of his fellow Americans, and even supplies him with reasons for strengthening the bonds by which others are excluded from even the merest comforts of human existence. Edwards was concerned with the unclean imaginations of his people, but we are living in a time when the imaginations of national glory fill the world with devastation. If there was any need for the languid will to exercise itself in the direction of beauty in the century of Jonathan Edwards, that need is enormously magnified in the century of the atomic bomb and the urban slum.

Edwards was an artist for his people, he was the reporter and the critic who caused them to focus on the larger world. His sermons were designed to terrify. They were for his time what Picasso's "Guernica" is for ours. They are Eisenstein's films of war and revolution, they are the photographs of police dogs and sheriff's deputies in Alabama, or the television report of American soldiers setting fire to the straw huts of Asian peasants. The earth over which we walk is no less rotten than it was for those who were in the hearing of Jonathan Edwards that unforgettable day in Enfield, Connecticut. "The arrows of death," he reminded them in July of 1741, "fly unseen at noonday. The sharpest sight cannot discern them." What man among us, 222 years later, on that unforgettable day in the November of 1963, could have thought otherwise?

In these sermons Edwards was not wandering off the edge of a realistic mentality into a foolish other-worldliness: rather, he was bringing his hearers out of their irrelevant and fruitless Sunday musings, and showing on the seachart of their lives as a people precisely where they were and precisely whither they were bound. What Jonathan Edwards preached and wrote in all of his sermons was a radical this-worldliness. It is for this reason that the failure of Jonathan Edwards is a fact of no small significance in the American civilization. After Edwards every great American prophet would fail in the same way. The American journey is over. Let the dream of the ultimate society be spoken in public ceremonies, but never dispatch the will and the intelligence in the active attempt to achieve it. The ship is at anchor, the sails down. There will be many men who will with great usefulness labor at tightening her rigging, cleaning her decks, and keeping the logs of her once great adventures. But there is no captain at the wheel, and too few crewmen athirst for the open sea.

X.

AND THE PRESS
SHALL GROAN
IN WILD TARTARY

O ne of the most poignantly revealing documents in all of the Edwards literature is the letter he wrote to the Princeton trustees five months before his death. He was obviously deeply touched by the invitation to become president of the college after his seven years of isolation and obscurity in the Indian mission at Stockbridge. But characteristically, he begins his reply to the invitation with a straightforward account of the obstacles to his acceptance. First, there is the matter of money. He acknowledges indirectly that the move from Northampton to the wilderness left them near destitution; another move would be possible only if there were a more generous recompense.

"But this is not my main objection," he admits. The chief difficulties are two. The first is what he considered to be his precarious health. As we noted above, he complained that his solids were "flaccid" and his fluids "sizy and scarce." But more important than his health is "that engaging in this business will not well consist with those views, and that course of employ in my study, which have long engaged and swal-

lowed up my mind, and been the chief entertainment and delight of my life."[1] Here is an unusually frank admission on
the part of a man who all along knew his major responsibilities
to lie in the public life of his people. It is at his desk with pen
in hand, he painfully explains to the trustees, that his passions
are in fullest exercise. And now, surging toward expression in
his mental reflection are several great works he is desirous of
publishing. One of these seems in particular to have a powerful hold on his present thinking.

> I have had on my mind and heart, (which I long ago be-
> gan, not with any view to publication,) a great work, which
> I call a *History of the Work of Redemption,* a body of
> divinity in an entire new method, being thrown into the
> form of a history; considering the affair of Christian The-
> ology, as the whole of it, in each part, stands in reference
> to the great work of redemption by Jesus Christ.[2]

This history will begin in eternity and descend from there into
the circuitous path of the people of God through this world
torn as it is by revolutions. The great narrative will not conclude until the last judgment "when it shall be said, *It is done.
I am Alpha and Omega, the Beginning and the End."* Finally,
describing the great volume which he was never to write, he
remarks significantly that this "entire new method" of doing
theology is a "method which appears to me the most beautiful
and entertaining, wherein every divine doctrine will appear
to the greatest advantage, in the brightest light, in the most
striking manner, shewing the admirable contexture and harmony of the whole."[3]

If Edwards' death was to interrupt the execution of this
grand project, there was to follow him no other human being
who possessed the genius or the ambition or the inventiveness

[1] Faust, Clarence H., and Thomas H. Johnson, eds., *Jonathan Edwards* (New
York, 1962), p. 410.
[2] *Ibid.,* p. 411.   [3] *Ibid.,* p. 412.

to do it in his stead. Religious and philosophical men in our century have talked voluminously of the interpenetration of the historical and spiritual sciences, but none has dared attempt a history that was simultaneously a theology, nor a theology that was simultaneously a history. Such a radically "entire new method" remains to be done. Men still write history as though they were attempting to unearth and expose the events and experiences of seasons past as they actually occurred, but they rarely take into their narrative the vagaries of their own personal history through which the past is being viewed. Should an Asian Maoist, a British Oxonian, and a white South African, all well-educated and intelligent, undertake the writing of an "objective" world history, there is little doubt that the areas of agreement in the "factual" reportage would be limited if not non-existent. On the other hand, men still explore the human soul, dissecting the manner by which it attains beliefs and exercises affections, with the dullest sensitivity to the past and future histories by which any particular soul is shaped. Jonathan Edwards thought it was his office to put these two tasks together.

Having followed Edwards' intellectual journey to its end, we should have gained for ourselves a relatively clear understanding of how he would have proceeded in the achievement of this great project. We have learned that there are no effectual operations occurring within the soul of a man that do not make themselves visible in the shape of his life. But visibility, as Edwards well understood, is a relative matter. A man is not visible to himself; but only to another. A man is visible only insofar as he is *seen* by other men, or as Edwards preferred to put it, only so far as he is "apparent" to others. We are concerned here with what causes one man to take notice of another. Why is it that the presence of some persons is more noticeable than others? Edwards would surely have recognized something of his own thinking in the critics of modern American society who have spoken passionately of the "invisible man," a man who is simply ignored and not taken account of, a man whose life makes no difference. The invisible man is a man who has no history.

Since this is a point of the greatest importance in our understanding of Edwards it is prudent to pause here to walk slowly around it for a moment. A minimum definition of history would have it to be an account of what is visible in the lives of human beings. When we write the history of a man we are stating what it is about that particular person that has become apparent to us. There is much we leave out. Unless he was a wrestler or a jungle explorer, we do not talk much about his weight or his physical cunning; and unless he became visible by the peculiarities of his social habits, we do not talk about his manner of dress or the accent he had acquired. We are concerned in our history to tell of those things in a man that have influenced others. This influence can, of course, vary greatly. There are truly few men who have significantly altered the circumstances under which others must live, and it is of such men that we write our histories, or tell them. We should not suppose that the most important histories are those which become the subject of classroom lectures. Indeed, these may be the most trivial. A man will tell with the greatest liveliness that which is of the greatest importance to his own life. Therefore, the lives of the persons who count most in the teller's own personal future are those whose histories we should most often hear from him. A girl may spend three hours a week hearing in well-organized detail a careful account of the growth of mercantilism in Northern Europe, but be moved to repeat none of it except as it can survive in her memory long enough to be transcribed onto an examination paper. At the same time, she may want to talk for hours about the personal characteristics of her professor since, as she believes or perhaps dreams, there are chances she will succeed in her romantic designs on him. A schoolboy will find no eagerness for memorizing the American presidents, but he might be able to repeat without hesitation an abundance of facts and statistics about the performance of his favorite baseball team. In the truest sense, then, history is not primarily concerned with the events in another man's past as they are in themselves, but only as they give life and dimension to one's own present life. The reasons for this are not far to seek. A person will follow with far deeper enthusiasm those directions which he believes will lead to the most numerous new possibilities for his life. The girl has convinced herself that the alternative which promises the greatest richness is not acquiring a respectable knowledge of academic history, but marrying the professor. The schoolboy knows that little awaits him for the successful memorization of his lessons. But to be a great athlete!

A person will remain invisible to us if he does not appear to have the possibility of taking a decisive part in the shaping of our own future. On the same account, the degree of that person's visibility will vary according to the degree to which our life depends on his. To the man about to make a proposal of marriage, the girl he hopes will become his wife will be far more visible to him than any other, and his most enlivened talk will be about her. To the athlete will be particularly visible the speed and strength of his opponent, to the soldier the courage of his enemy, to the student the generosity of his professor, to the slave the heroism of his liberator.

Therefore, when histories are told we know much about the teller, for he tells of himself as much as of another. We know what the present circumstances of his life mean to him, and where he expects his life to be more abundant, if he expects anything at all. To know a man's hero is to know that man's soul. To hear the histories a man tells is to have him make himself apparent to you. If a man can tell no histories, if there is no one who can cause his life to be abundant, then there is no life in that man. Nothing of him has become visible because there is nothing in him. If a man has few heroes, but tells of himself as though he were a hero, it is because he is terrified that there is no life in him.

Here, then, is the question with which we must return to Edwards: How shall we write the history of the visible saints? First, we would have to know what expectations the believer has for his own life. Certainly, one of the features of the doctrine of immortality that made it so attractive to Edwards was that it can be used to show the infinite expectations the believer has for his own life. The visible saint is so filled with life that the finitude of the world never seems to destroy the infinite possibilities that lie ever before him. Edwards has also talked about the nature of the believer's expectations in the trinity and God's last end, for there we learned that the life of the saint is not only infinite in length, but also in depth, since the whole meaning and purpose of all that is can be expressed in a single act of the will. He has said the believer's expectations are infinite in the doctrine of the union with Christ, and in the treatise on the affections, for there we learned that the soul of the saint is possessed of a tireless vitality and love, inasmuch as Christ dwells "savingly" within as a "new simple idea." We have, then, only to hear him say it in the form of a history, an "entire new method" of expressing all these doctrines.

As noted above, the grand history Edwards talked about in his 1757 letter to the Princeton trustees was never written. There is, however, an interesting collection of material composed much earlier, apparently before the idea for this history had taken firm shape in his thinking. In his letter he refers to this work "which I long ago began, not with any view to publication." This is a series of sermons preached in Northampton in 1739, and which lay in manuscript until 1773 when his son made them available to the printer. Jonathan

Edwards Jr. accurately described them as mere "outlines" of that greater projected work and warned that "the reader cannot reasonably expect all that from them, which he might justly have expected, had they been written with such a view, and prepared by the author's own hand for the press."[4] But, perhaps appropriately, the younger Edwards gave it the title his father had thought to give the unwritten work: *A History of the Work of Redemption.*

These sermons do indeed bear all the marks of a hasty execution. Themes are begun and not continued. There are few surprises in the narrative, and rarely is there an illuminating insight. The account slavishly follows the scriptural narrative where there is one, but where periods of world history are omitted in the Old Testament, he feels no restraint in filling out those omissions by his own speculation. This material certainly fails the test by which he thought this "great work" should be distinguished: it is hardly "beautiful and entertaining, wherein every divine doctrine will appear to the greatest advantage, in the brightest light." Surely Edwards felt this way about it himself, for there is no mention anywhere of his intention to see the 1739 document into print. And yet by adapting our interpretive procedure to its limitations, we can make a reasonable guess as to what Edwards might have written had there been time enough and strength.

He undertakes to tell a story that is nothing less than an eternal drama, involving as a cast the whole of the trinity along with the whole of mankind. His subject matter is all

> that Christ does in this great affair as mediator, in any of his offices, either of prophet, priest, or king; either when he was in this world, in his human nature, or before, or since; and not only what Christ the mediator has done, but also what the Father, or the Holy Ghost, have done, as united or confederated in this design of redeeming sinful

[4] *Works,* (see Chap. One, note 7), p. 296.

men; or, in one word, all that is wrought in execution of the eternal covenant of redemption.[5]

The first act opens on the dark moment of Adam's fall. No sooner did this happen, Edwards tells us, than

> Christ the eternal Son of God clothed himself with the mediatorial character, and therein presented himself before the Father. He immediately stepped in between a holy, infinite, offended majesty, and offending mankind; and was accepted in his interposition; and so wrath was prevented from going forth in the full execution of that amazing curse that man had brought on himself.[6]

It is interesting to note how Edwards finds evidence of the beginning of Christ's redemptive work in these early biblical episodes. Genesis 3:15 had long been referred to by the church as the "proto-evangellion" since it was thought that when God cursed the serpent for deceiving Eve he was therewith promising victory in his warfare against the forces of evil. As Edwards reads these words he finds that they cause something to *appear* to Adam and Eve. There was "a certain intimation of the light of the sun in the east when the day first dawns."[7] Soon after this he tells us the custom of sacrificing was appointed. Sacrifice was also a work of Christ accomplished by its *appearance* to the saints, for "it tended to establish in the minds of God's visible church, the necessity of a propitiatory sacrifice, in order to the Deity's being satisfied for sin."[8]

By so appearing to the first persons of this earth, God was saving them. Adam and Eve were saved, and so was Abel. As we follow the scriptural narrative there is a marked progress in the work of redemption. In the days of Enos there is a special outpouring of the Spirit. Then we come upon Enoch who "was a saint of greater eminency than any ever had been

[5] *Works*, I, 299.   [6] *Works*, I, 306.   [7] *Works*, I, 308f.
[8] *Works*, I, 311.

before him; so that in this respect the work of redemption was carried on to a greater height than ever it had been before."[9] There is then the problem of interpreting the flood, for in it were destroyed all but Noah and his family. This is nonetheless an advance for the work of redemption, Edwards decides, since "God removed out of the way the enemies and obstacles of it, that were ready to overthrow it."[10] Moreover, with the flood there was a new covenant of grace made with Noah and through him with his descendants.[11] God promised "to destroy the earth in like manner no more; signifying how it is by the sacrifice of Christ that God's favor is obtained."[12] This renewal of the covenant marks the beginning of a new period, or dispensation, in God's plan, which continues apace until the idolatry of God's people causes him to renew the covenant again—this time with Abraham.

This new expression of the covenant is sufficient from the time of Abraham to the time of Moses; then from Moses to David there is another dispensation; and from David to the Babylonian exile. The final period of preparation is that which lies between the exile and the incarnation. In this last period Edwards apparently feels that the paucity of information available in scripture allows him to wander into other sources of knowledge about the history of that period of the world. From scripture he charts the final preparation of the people of God, now humiliated before all the principalities of the world by their exile; so that with their pride sufficiently mortified, they were ready for Christ. From other sources he opines that the world, too, was thoroughly prepared. The four great revolutions—Babylonian, Assyrian, Greek and Roman—that swept over the world "like the four winds striving together on the tumultuous raging ocean," will show us that "all things are ready for the birth of Christ."[13] This is the end of the first

9 *Works*, I, 314.   10 *Works*, I, 318.   11 *Works*, I, 319.
12 *Works*, I, 320.   13 *Works*, I, 388.

act. The curtain has fallen on a scene of great confusion. Our heroes—the people of the visible church—are nearly lost from view. At least there is no certainty that they will survive the onslaught of the raging armies of darkness.

The second act opens on the birth of Christ, an event of such defenseless innocence that it is conspicuous for that reason alone. We have already reviewed the character of this period, which begins with the incarnation and ends with the resurrection, and we learned that it is here that the struggle of the light against the darkness, however feeble it might have seemed in the previous centuries, promises victory for the armies of peace. No longer does the visible church of the Old Testament appear to be a splinter group of true believers who receive little more than the hatred of the world as a reward for their faithfulness. Now they appear to be the gallant advance guard in the establishment of a new age for mankind. They are not an insignificant handful of men who perished in some past history, they are the men who have made possible an altogether new history. This is what we learn in the story of Christ when we set it in the greater sequence of events. Now the saints can see that they are under a valiant captain in whose command victory is certain. The curtain falls with the death of Christ, but it is a death in which the observer can be convinced that evil has had its most severe exercise, so he looks eagerly to the beginning of the next and final act.

The third act is by far the most exciting in Edwards' conception of it, for it is here that the final combat is undertaken, here that the actual victory is achieved. More importantly, it is here that the actors leave the stage and come forward, and all the observers join in the drama. The curtain rises on Christ as he takes his position for the coming action.

In order that Christ might carry on the work of redemption, and accomplish the success of his own purchase as God-man, it was necessary that he should be alive, and so that he should rise from the dead. Therefore, Christ, after he had finished this purchase by death, and by continuing for a time under the power of death, rises from the dead, to fulfill the end of his purchase, and himself to bring about that for which he died.[14]

After rising from the dead, he ascends into heaven and sits on the right hand of the Father. Edwards is most explicit about this.

> And as he ascended into heaven, God the Father did in a visible manner set him on the throne as king of the universe. He then put the angels all under him, and subjected heaven and earth under him, that he might govern them for the good of the people for whom he had died.[15]

With Christ in possession of life and power the church was then given the necessary means of success for its struggle in the world. The Jewish dispensation was ended; after Christ the Jewish dispensation was not adequate, since the people of God were no longer to consist of one nation, but would rather be taken from all the nations of the world. Then the Christian sabbath was established; the gospel ministry appointed and sent forth; the apostles were endowed with extraordinary gifts of healing and prophecy; all those things were revealed which had been hidden in the Old Testament; Paul was converted; councils were convened; and finally the New Testament was committed to writing.[16]

Now that the visible people of God are equipped with all the weaponry necessary for their visible victory in the world, they proceed at once to battle with Christ at their head, for the Antichrist is already in the field. In the first encounter the church achieves some gain with the fall of Jerusalem in 68 A.D., but now "the devil turns his hand elsewhere, and uses

[14] *Works,* I, 431.   [15] *Works,* I, 433.
[16] *Works,* I, 434ff.

other instruments."[17] These instruments are the pagan learning and the political power of the Roman Empire which were exercised against the Christians with great fury until the time of Constantine's conversion in 320. But Satan's employment of the Roman Empire was ended with the emperor's seizing on Christ, and for a while there was great peace accompanied by the remarkable scenes of the heathen emperors, princes and generals who had persecuted the Christians, "dying miserably, one and another, under exquisite torments of body, and horrors of conscience, with a most visible hand of God upon them."[18]

But Satan was still not undone; he turned now to the church and began to infest that. "The Arians began soon after Constantine came to the throne." Then in the next century he appeared in the Pelagian heresy, and in the apostasy of Julian. So the respite was brief, "as it were *for half an hour,* wherein the four angels held the four winds from blowing, till the servants of God should be sealed in their foreheads."[19] By the time of the Reformation the success of the Antichrist had been almost complete. But then "God began gloriously to revive his church again, and advance the kingdom of his Son, after such a dismal night of darkness as had been before from the rise of Antichrist to that time."[20] Although Satan was severely attacked in this period he responded vigorously with the Council of Trent, then with savage warfare, persecution, and corrupt opinions.[21]

As Edwards draws close to the present day in his narrative he notes a certain series of encouraging signs: there is a growth of Christianity in Muscovy, an extensive propagation of the gospel in America, and also in Malabar. But all in all, there has been about as much gain in the years since the Reformation as there has been loss. The Reformed church has diminished and morals have disintegrated.[22] However, on the other

[17] *Works*, I, 445. [18] *Works*, I, 449. [19] *Works*, I, 454.
[20] *Works*, I, 462. [21] *Works*, I, 463. [22] *Works*, I, 470.

hand, the power of the Pope has also faded; there is less persecution now than there was, and there is a great increase in
learning.[23] What therefore does the future hold?

One of the most significant features of Edwards' historical
account of the time remaining between the present and the
end is that for him there will be a kingdom established on
earth, before the church is glorified in heaven. It is toward
that end that the current growth in religion is tending, but
the imminent "pouring out of the Spirit of God will not
effect the overthrow of Satan's visible kingdom, till there has
first been a violent and mighty opposition made."[24] There will
be a final struggle between these two visible kingdoms "called
the battle of the great day of God Almighty." The armies in
this great battle will be made up of those who are on the sides
of Christ or Satan. And everyone will be on one side or another; there will be no "neuters." But the outcome is not un-
certain: "Christ and his church shall in this battle obtain a
complete and entire victory over their enemies."[25] There is,
of course, no diminution of the historical nature of this period.
It will be the same world with the same dimensions; but a
world without evil. It will be a time of great light and knowledge. "It may be hoped, that then many of the Negroes and
Indians will be divines, and that excellent books will be published in Africa, in Ethiopia, in Tartary, and other of now the
most barbarous countries."[26] It will be a time of great holiness.
"Religion shall not be an empty profession as it now mostly is,
but holiness of heart and life shall abundantly prevail."[27] There
will be peace and love everywhere; wars between nations will
be replaced with good understanding. "Then shall all the
world be united in one amiable society."[28] In another work
Edwards says it is a modest estimate that at the end of this

[23] *Works*, I, 471.   [24] *Works*, I, 483.   [25] *Works*, I, 484.
[26] *Works*, I, 491.   [27] *Works*, I, 492.   [28] *Works*, I, 493.

period the number of converts on earth will have been multiplied by some 100,000.[29]

It would appear that Edwards spent many pleasant hours in his study musing over the delights of life in the visible kingdom of Christ on earth. There are frequent references to the "Millenium" in the miscellaneous notes.

how happy will that state be when neither divine nor human learning shall be confined and imprisoned within only two or three nations of Europe, but shall be diffused all over the world and this lower world shall be all over covered with light the various parts of it mutually enlightening each other. . . . and the press shall groan in wild Tartary.[30]

We are repeatedly reminded that spiritual blessings will not be enlarged without corresponding gains in the secular realm.

Tis probable that this world shall be more like heaven in the millenium in this respect, that contemplative & spiritual employments, and those things that more directly concern the mind & religion will be more the saints ordinary business than now. There will be so many contrivances and inventions to facilitate and expedite their necessary secular business that they shall have more time for more nobler exercises . . . the invention of the mariners compass is one thing by God discovered to the world for that end, and how exceedingly has that one thing enlarged and facilitated communication. And who can tell but that God will yet make it more perfect so that there need not be such a tedious voyage in order to hear from the other hemisphere & and so the countries about the poles need no longer to lie hid to us but the whole earth may be as one community one body in X.[31]

[29] "An Humble Attempt to Promote Explicit Agreement and Visible Union of God's People in Extraordinary Prayer," *Works*, III, 449.
[30] *Miscellanies*, Yale MSS., No. 26.
[31] *Miscellanies*, Yale MSS., No. 262.

But the earthly millennium will not last forever. We do not know how long it will be exactly: scripture says only that it will be a long time.[32] We do know that just "before the end of the world, there shall be a very great apostasy, wherein great parts of the world shall fall away from Christ and his church."

> Satan shall begin to set up his dominion again in the world. This world shall again become a scene of darkness and wickedness. The bottomless pit of hell shall be opened, and devils shall come up again out of it, and a dreadful smoke shall ascend to darken the world. And the church of Christ, instead of extending to the utmost bounds of the world, as it did before, shall be reduced to narrow limits again.[33]

In the midst of this great tribulation "Christ will appear in the glory of his Father, with all his holy angels, coming in the clouds of heaven." This coming will be unexpected by the wicked; for them "it will come as a cry at midnight: they shall be taken in the midst of their wickedness, and it will give them a dreadful alarm. It will at once break upon their revels, their eating, and drinking, and carousing."[34]

In numerous sermons and miscellaneous notes Edwards dispatches his imagination in search of terms by which the magnificence of this scene can be depicted.

> We can now conceive but little of the holy and awful magnificence in which Christ will appear, as he shall come in the clouds of heaven, or of the glory of his retinue. How mean and despicable, in comparison with it, is the most splendid appearance that earthly princes can make! A glorious visible light will shine round about him, and the earth, with all nature, will tremble at his presence. How vast and innumerable will that host be which will appear with him! Heaven will be for the time deserted of its inhabitants.[35]

---

[32] *Works,* I, 494.   [33] *Works,* I, 495.   [34] *Works,* I, 498.
[35] "The Final Judgment," *Works,* IV, 210f.

But the stage will nonetheless be the earth, and the eyes with which we behold the drama will be eyes of flesh; and the Christ who appears will come with his human nature intact. "Christ will thus descend into our air, to such a distance from the surface of the earth, that every one, when all shall be gathered together, shall see him."[36]

Then in the course of this spectacle "the last trumpet shall sound, and the dead shall be raised, and the living changed."[37] The graves will be emptied, the earth and the sea shall give up their dead. The souls which until this time have been in heaven will descend with Christ, and those which have been in hell will ascend to earth, and all will be restored to their bodies. Even those bodies which were scattered by fire, and those which were eaten by beasts or fishes, will be united with their souls. Through all of this the wicked will be trying vainly to escape or to hide; they will "cry to the mountains to fall on them."[38] But the saints will mount up greatly in joy, for they will perceive how their redemption is becoming increasingly complete: for now, rejoined to their bodies, they are redeemed in *both* soul and body; for now for the first time the *whole* church of Christ is brought visibly together in one place.[39]

Now the entire cast is assembled on the vast stage of the last day of history. All things and persons are visible. All truths are known. Nothing new can happen. Here we are surprised to learn that the third act does not end. The world will perish in flame but the souls of all men will continue to live forever in blessedness or anguish. The history of faith, Edwards is saying, is without a conclusion. Seasons will come and go, periods of time will begin and end, but the drama of life and faith is open-ended and will never be exhausted.

36 *Works*, IV, 211.
37 "History of Redemption," *Works*, I, 499.
38 "The Final Judgment," *Works*, IV, 212f.
39 "History of Redemption," *Works*, I, 500f.

Here, then, is Edwards' history of the visible saints. It scarcely need be said that its treatment of what is commonly regarded by the academic mentality as "historical fact" is less than adequate. But let us here push this history back into our earlier analysis of what the term "history" can be taken to mean. What do we learn about Edwards from the history he tells? We learn that his heroes are neither physical nor intellectual giants who could stand off the gathered hostilities of the pagan world. They are not men and women who war against Satan with the weapons of Satan. They are rather a people who are attempting to bring light into the darkness by the very design of their actual lives.

Let us remember, at the same time, Edwards was not telling this history solely for himself. He was not concerned to have others see that his heroes had infinite expectations for their own lives; but he wanted rather to demonstrate by his history the expectations he held for his own life and for the lives of his people. The 1739 sermons are an imperfect attempt at such a grand history, but they do indicate how he thought it could be achieved. We observe that, among its other peculiarities, this history does not stop with the present. The usual academic history has a conclusion somewhere in time. Moreover, before the long chronicle is finished the Northampton congregation is made aware that the people whose arduous path through the centuries has been told is none but the very church in Northampton. It is their own history they are listening to. It is their own circumstances that they hear being described, it is the dimensions of their own lives, the origin and outcome of their own personal values, that they hear spoken from the pulpit. My heroes are not the men of the past, their preacher is calling out a century after John Winthrop's words to his heroes somewhere on the Atlantic Ocean, but you, the people of this congregation and of this land, you are my heroes.

Staring up at their preacher were the several hundred faces

of men and women whose lives were stirred by as many different kinds of expectations. There were farmers, their beautiful hands lying half-open on their laps, who were never quite sure they had caught the meaning of the preacher's fine English. There were women for whom the Sabbath service was the one moment in the week when they were far enough from the demands of children and husbands that they could silently appraise the precariousness and tragedy that marbled the lives they never had a choice but to live. There were newly-established merchants, carpenters and masons, for whose touch the hard permanence of coin had become so familiar that they could safely develop a hard permanence of opinion. There were the young men and the lean scrubbed girls whose dreams could rewrite any of the thousand histories passing invisibly through them. There were the old women, and here and there an old man, bent and deaf to all histories.

Before them all stood the man who thought he could make God visible to his age. While he delivered these sermons in 1739, he was momentarily convinced he would succeed. As his narrative passed through Northampton he took the faces before him on across the battlefields of his imagination which, no doubt, he thought he could see in his own lifetime. The heroes within the range of his voice would themselves one day be so excitingly visible in the world, he thought, that others would press eagerly to join in the making of their history. Knowledge would fill the world, turnpikes would cut their ribbons across chemically enriched farmland and giant vessels would navigate the heavens. And the press, cried Jonathan Edwards, the press would groan in wild Tartary.

But the Jonathan Edwards who stood in the pulpit of Northampton told the wrong history; he failed to translate his own expectations into the life of his congregation. Therefore, our judgment must be harsh. He had asked that the faith of a man be proved authentic by its visibility, by its beauty. Jonathan Edwards, in the final weighing, was not beautiful in the telling of his histories. It is true that for a brief, all too brief, moment he caused the Spirit to pass through Northampton and on into New England. But the inheritance was wind.

Jonathan Edwards was a philosopher, an intellectual. He knew he should be engaged in the public issues of the day, but he was never fully engaged. As he admitted obliquely to the Princeton trustees, he really preferred to all other entertainments, the cerebrations of his own genius. There were exceptional moments, in the thirties especially, when he went forth and truly looked into the lives of his people and patiently listened to them. But even then he was enormously busy with himself. It is reported that returning from his pastoral calls there would be notes pinned about on his cloak, ideas scribbled down at the moment they came to him and affixed to his person that they might never be lost. It is for this reason that Edwards the pastor, the public man, the visible Jonathan Edwards, was never beautiful to his people: he never lost a thought, but, especially in the latter years of his ministry, he let many a person float silently to the ground unattended by his affection. By temperament and character Edwards was usually stern and sober, he was easily distracted, inclined to be aloof, and, most unfortunate of all, he was petty and womanish in his moral judgments. He could write elegantly direct statements about the sublime excellency of the ethical life, but there was nothing in his visible mien that served as a commanding model for the "consent of being to being." It is possible that no one will ever write a more reasonable and perceptive essay on the distinctions between gracious affections and false, but when Edwards was finally required to make those distinctions he was awkward and unlovely.

*   *   *

When Edwards died in 1758 at the age of 55, the political establishment of the nation lay thirty years beyond him. Desires for national independence had not yet been ignited, since the crown still had not challenged the economic independence of the colonies. There had been no effort in America to develop a philosophy of constitutional government. Lockean metaphysics and epistemology had long been studied in the colleges, but Locke's political thought lay sleeping, waiting to be awakened by Tom Jefferson who at the time of Edwards' death was only in his sixteenth year.

The first great soldiers and statesmen of the American nation were, in Edwards' last decade, men still driven by the dreams and adventures of youth; they had not yet set their lives upon that single design which alone could win a war and establish a nation. Washington was born in 1732, a year after Edwards' first public appearance before the New England clergy in Boston. By 1758 he had won something of a reputation as an officer in the militia of the governor of Virginia, having none too skillfully, but successfully, defended the Virginia border against the French. In that year he quit his soldiering and took a new wife to Mount Vernon certain that by the gentlemanly management of his estate and casual participation in the government of Virginia he could hold the world at bay.

Benjamin Franklin was Edwards' junior by only three years, but he would survive him by thirty-two. Rich and famous from his writings and from his commercial enterprises, Franklin's political thinking through 1758 was still undeveloped, if only for the absence of practical necessity. The uncommon blessing of long age and health brought Franklin that necessity, and in the last three decades of his life he met it with a genius not wholly evident by 1758.

Neither Edwards himself nor his writings were to play an important part in the final shaping of the government which Americans erected within their civilization near the end of its second century. We shall seriously misinterpret the life and thought of Jonathan Edwards if we expect to find in him the marks of a devoted patriot, or even the primitive design of a

new political system. Edwards left no institution, no movement, no religious or philosophical teachings that would have
significant influence on subsequent generations. He was, of
course, an important figure in the Great Awakening, a movement of the people in which the Spirit of Nationalism was to
sow more than the Spirit of Christ; but the Great Awakening did not need Edwards to open it, nor did he succeed in
properly closing it. A handful of theological motifs were kept
alive by several decades of "Edwardeans," but as time passed
his spiritual descendants seemed little more than the defenders of a tired orthodoxy; they were no longer sensitive to the
subtle but decisive emendations the Calvinist tradition underwent at Edwards' hand.

The fascination of Jonathan Edwards, and his significance,
lie in quite another place. What becomes visible in the history
of this man is the very character of America itself. Like Americans in every age he understood the past to be nothing less
than a preparation for the future; and he understood the
present to consist in efforts to achieve that future. That this
soil was the place on which the kingdom of Christ would be
first established was not an idea of Edwards' own invention.
It had been carried across the "Attlantick" a hundred years
before he heard of it. Nor did this idea need Edwards to fix
itself in the American imagination. It was soon to be secu-
larized, and often trivialized, as the dream of a perfect society,
a nation where the noblest of human aspirations could be met.
American statesmen and poets would call their nation to receive the starved and the huddled masses of the world; they
would dispatch its power abroad to guarantee the freedoms of
men elsewhere. America, in Lincoln's words, is "the last best
hope of earth."

Like Americans in every age Edwards also understood that
the glories of the future would not be attained without the
sustained labor of the present. Not by their oral profession,

but by what they actually do, will Americans bring their light into the world. But it was Jonathan Edwards who, more clearly than anyone before or since, put the future together with the present; he judged men's actions according to their effectiveness in bringing us to the ultimate society. He found them wanting, and, in words not soon to be forgotten, he said so. The failure of Jonathan Edwards is not therefore just the story of an eighteenth century church at the western edge of an English colony. When two hundred and thirty male members of the Northampton church indicated by vote that they did not want to be judged according to the gap that lay between their oral profession and the efforts actually to live their lives by it, they spoke for the American civilization itself.

Edwards had a century in which to test the viability of John Winthrop's vision; we have had two centuries to test Edwards'. He knew the American journey would be treacherous, but we know it much more vividly. We know that when the press does groan in wild Tartary, when ships do navigate the heavens and there are no delays in the transmission of knowledge from one continent to another, men still do not "consent to being in general," they still "love those who are of their own party, and who are warmly engaged on their side." But however difficult appears the American journey, however inclined Americans are toward "dull and lifeless wouldings" for everything except their own self-interest, nothing is taken from the force of Edwards' understanding of the way the American dream is to be brought to reality. There must appear in our midst, he thought, a smaller society of men and women whose visible lives will be marked by such beauty that they can become for our civilization its most apparent good. For then the history of the lives of this people would become the reason for a nation to resume its pilgrimage. Edwards would have called these men and women the people of God. But if such a people does not appear, there is no God, and no ultimate society—only an inevitable victory for the powers of darkness.

A CHRONOLOGY OF THE LIFE AND WRITINGS
OF JONATHAN EDWARDS

1703	Jonathan Edwards is born, October 5, in East Windsor, Connecticut, the only son of eleven children born to Timothy and Esther Stoddard Edwards.
1715	Writes "Of Insects," an essay on the Balloon, or Flying, Spider, revealing a precocious ability to observe and describe natural phenomena.
1716	Enters Yale College in his thirteenth year.
1719–20	In his senior year Edwards writes the "Notes on the Mind," a miscellaneous collection of observations on a number of philosophical topics. Here we see his critical appreciation of the philosophy of John Locke, and his ability as an independent thinker.
1720	Graduates from Yale College.
1720–22	Undertakes graduate study in theology at Yale. During his second year he experiences his conversion, or what he later called "a new sense of things."
1722–23	For eight months he serves as pastor of a Presbyterian church in New York City.
1724–26	Takes up the office of Tutor at Yale College during a period of controversy for the college, and spiritual trial for himself.
1726	Agrees to be an assistant to his grandfather, Solomon Stoddard, minister of the church in Northampton, Massachusetts. Stoddard's preeminence among the New England clergy had been secured some twenty years earlier by his victory over Cotton Mather in the Half-Way Covenant debate. The Half-Way Covenant, a weakened American version of the old Puritan principle of visible sainthood, was effectively abandoned after Stoddard attacked its inconsistency.
1727	Edwards marries Sarah Pierrepont of New Haven who "is of a wonderful sweetness, calmness and universal benevolence of mind," and who was to bear him twelve children.
1729	Solomon Stoddard dies at the age of 85 and Edwards becomes the senior minister.
1731	In Boston, at the invitation of the clergy of that city, Edwards delivers the sermon, "God Glorified in the Work of Redemption by the Greatness of Man's Dependence upon Him in the Whole of it," his first published work. This date marks Edwards' first public appearance before the theological world of New England, and the beginning of the most successful decade of his ministry.

1734   Edwards preaches "A Divine and Supernatural Light, Immediately Imparted to the Soul by the Spirit of God," one of his best known sermons, and "The Excellency of Christ," a theological masterpiece.

1735   The evangelical warmth of Edwards' sermons finally bears fruit in the first revival in Northampton during his ministry.

1737   Edwards' informal history of the 1735 revival, and one of the most influential of his books during his own lifetime, *A Faithful Narrative of the Surprising Work of God,* is published.

1738   John Taylor's popular attack of Calvinist doctrine, *The Scripture-Doctrine of Original Sin Proposed to a Free and Candid Examination,* is published.

1739   Edwards preaches the series of sermons to be published in 1773 as *The History of the Work of Redemption.*

1740   The evangelist, George Whitefield, arrives from England, setting off the Great Awakening. Edwards is soon prominent in this widespread revival.

1741   As a guest preacher at Enfield, Connecticut, Edwards delivers "Sinners in the Hands of an Angry God," the most famous sermon of the Great Awakening. In the same year he writes *The Distinguishing Marks of a Work of the Spirit of God,* indicating his concern that there not be more heat than light in this vigorous season of the spirit.

1742   Edwards publishes more reflections on the events of the day: *Some Thoughts concerning the Present Revival of Religion in New England.*

1742–43   With the noise of the Awakening still ringing in his ears Edwards preaches a series of sermons on the problem of determining whether religious affections are truly gracious. These were to be published in 1746 as the *Treatise concerning Religious Affections.*

1743   Charles Chauncy, Boston's great liberal preacher and Edwards' most important contemporary antagonist, publishes his *Seasonable Thought on the State of Religion in New England,* a detailed account of the excesses of the Awakening.

1743–48   A barren period in the church of Northampton during which a series of petty controversies begin to set church against minister.

1747   With an eye to the divisions of the world-wide church Edwards writes *An Humble Attempt to Promote Visible Union of God's People in Extraordinary Prayer for the Revival of Religion.* The death of David Brainerd in the Edwards home is followed in four months by the death of Brainerd's fiancee, and Edwards' daughter, Jerusha.

1748   Edwards raises the major issue of his life by arguing for a return to the old Puritan practice of admitting none but visible saints to church membership.

1749   Acknowledging a departure from the position his grandfather, Stoddard, had successfully defended a half-century before, Edwards publishes his *An Humble Inquiry into the Rules of God, concerning the Qualifications Requisite to a Complete Standing and Full Communion with the Visible Christian Church,* arguing for the necessity of the "church's Christian judgment" of the authenticity of a man's faith. The same year he also publishes David Brainerd's journal.

1750   On June 22 Edwards is relieved of his ministerial duties by a vote of 230 to 23. On July 2 he preaches his "Farewell Sermon" stating, without rancor, that Christ is the final judge of all men.

1751   Edwards becomes minister of the church in Stockbridge and missionary to the Indians. Until 1757 his removal from a busy community and heavy pastoral duties provides him time for the great theological projects he had long planned.

1754   *A Careful and Strict Enquiry into the Modern Prevailing Notions of that Freedom of Will which is Supposed to be Essential to Moral Agency, Vertue and Vice, Reward and Punishment, Praise and Blame* is published. This book, the best known of all of Edwards' works, is a summary of his lifelong opposition to the Arminian doctrine of free will.

1755   Writes "The Nature of True Virtue" and "Concerning the End for which God Created the World." These essays are to be published in 1765 as *Two Dissertations*.

1757   Edwards is chosen by the Princeton trustees to succeed his son-in-law, Aaron Burr, as president of the college.

1758   *The Great Christian Doctrine of Original Sin Defended*, a long delayed answer to John Taylor's 1738 book on sin, is published. In January Edwards assumes office as president, and on March 22 he dies of a smallpox innocculation.

INDEX